The Thrifty Gardener

Quarto

First published in 2026 by Frances Lincoln,
an imprint of The Quarto Group.
One Triptych Place, London, SE1 9SH,
United Kingdom
T (0)20 7700 9000
www.Quarto.com

EEA Representation, WTS Tax d.o.o., Žanova ulica 3,
4000 Kranj, Slovenia
www.wts-tax.si

A catalogue record for this book is available from the British Library.

ISBN 978-1-83600-411-0
Ebook ISBN 978-1-83600-412-7

10 9 8 7 6 5 4 3 2 1

Design by Michelle Kliem

Editorial Director: Alice Graham
Senior Designer: Isabel Eeles
Senior Editor: Charlotte Frost
Senior Production Controller: Rohana Yusof
Publisher: Philip Cooper

Printed in Guangdong, China TT122025

MIX
Paper | Supporting responsible forestry
FSC® C016973
FSC www.fsc.org

Picture credits

*© **Sarah Cuttle** pp.7, 9, 11, 19-20, 22, 25, 27-31, 33, 35-45, 50-51, 53, 55 (below right), 57-58, 63, 65, 67, 69 (below), 70, 78-79, 81-83, 90-91, 93-95, 101, 103-104, 107, 109, 110 (below right), 111 (below left and right), 115, 118 (below left), 119 (below left and middle), 120 (below right), 121 (below right), 122 (below right), 124 (below right), 125, 128, 130 (below middle), 131, 133, 134-135, 136 (below middle and right), 137 (below right), 141-142, 145, 147, 149-150, 152-153, 155-157, 159-165, 167, 169-173, 175, 177, 179 (top left), 180-182, 183 (below left and right), 185.*

*© **Mark Lane Designs Ltd** pp.4, 12, 17, 18, 21, 47, 48, 55 (top and below left), 56, 66, 69 (top), 71, 77, 80, 85, 88, 102, 105, 110 (below left and middle), 111 (below middle), 112-113, 116-117, 118 (below middle and right), 119 (below right), 120 (below left and middle), 121 (below middle), 122 (below left and middle), 123, 124 (below left and middle), 126-127, 130 (below left and right), 132 (below left and middle), 137 (below left), 140, 178, 179 (top right and below), 183 (top).*

*© **GAP Garden** pp.26 and 31 (below).*

*© **Getty Images** pp.121 (below left), 132 (below right), 136 (below left), 137 (below middle).*

Mark Lane

The Thrifty Gardener

Reduce waste, spend wisely

FRANCES LINCOLN

Contents

INTRODUCTION

In a world of climate change and growing inflation, every gardener needs to reassess how they garden and how they spend their money. Even the most experienced gardeners crave a thriftier – less wasteful and more productive – way to garden. This book is full of valuable tips for anyone wanting to garden more sustainably and cost-effectively, while still achieving satisfying results. Whether you have a small balcony or a large garden, a community garden or an allotment, the principles of thriftier gardening apply universally, and should be seen from a sustainable point of view: a thrifty garden should also be an eco-friendly or biodiverse garden.

Beginners will benefit from learning how to make smart choices with limited resources. Instead of buying every shiny new tool or expensive plant, discover how to maximize your impact using readily available or repurposed materials. You will learn to start with a solid foundation, such as improving soil health with homemade compost or free organic matter like fallen leaves to make a soil conditioner, saving money on fertilizers.

Experienced gardeners who may already have a well-established garden or have taken on a new garden will find value in a thriftier approach by refining skills and cutting unnecessary expenses. You can explore techniques like seed saving, plant propagation, creating natural habitats and smart watering methods that reduce both waste and costs. By adopting these practices, you can elevate your gardening prowess while keeping an eye on your budget. With the right tools and approach, and a little design knowledge, you can still have a gorgeous garden of which you can be proud.

I want this book to speak to the growing number of eco-conscious individuals who wish to reduce their environmental footprint. With advice on recycling materials, conserving water, growing cover crops, following a no-dig approach and using organic methods, this book aligns with sustainable living values. It teaches you how to grow your own food and flowers without harming the planet, all while promoting biodiversity and wildlife-friendly practices.

By taking small steps, you will start making actionable plans. Don't rush in, be focused and realistic. The first year might not be very productive, but you'll have observed the seasons, planned your borders or raised beds, worked out what sort of soil you have and how you can improve it, and worked out how to slow down the wind and plan your planting based on how much sun your garden gets. As you learn more skills and your confidence grows, you'll be able to overcome any difficulties or problems as they arise. This way, your garden will become more productive and manageable, and as the years pass, you'll start to spend even less.

Trial and error and learning from your mistakes make a great gardener. With limited funds, you'll have to take your time, and this will result in a better-functioning and more robust outdoor space, especially when it comes to sustainability, being eco-friendly, creating a garden rich in biodiversity and welcoming wildlife into your garden.

Ultimately, this book is for anyone interested in gardening, whether for personal pleasure or contributing to the larger conversation about sustainability. It offers timeless, practical knowledge that encourages creativity, resilience and responsible stewardship of the environment – all while keeping gardening accessible and affordable.

Above Colourful, everyday items can be repurposed – perfect for herbs, fruits and vegetables.

The thrifty approach

Thriftier gardening is not about instant results. It will take time, but this is the joy of gardening. Start with a clear plan, and your garden will grow with you. Yet, remember that your needs and requirements will alter over time, so you'll need to be flexible and open to change. This is normal. Also, plant fatalities happen to all of us.

While a no-maintenance garden doesn't exist, there are plants that are easy-to-care-for, don't have a hefty price tag (especially when bought at the right time of year), are easy to propagate from and will be low-maintenance (see pages 98–137). Time is precious for any gardener, so an average-sized garden, 255-square metres (2,745 square feet) or tennis court size, should only need 3–5 hours a week to keep it looking its best and producing healthy plants.

Save money

Saving money and creating a sustainable garden will soon be second nature. Looking at your garden with fresh eyes will help you move forward and prevent you from stopping at the first (invariably money-related) hurdle. This book will help you use money wisely not wastefully. I know there is an urge to pop to a garden centre or nursery to buy plants, but I'll guide you by sharing what I've learned, especially when I was set free on my first garden, and give you easy, thrifty, creative solutions so that you can be a more resourceful and frugal good gardener.

By being cost-wise in the garden by recycling, reusing and upcycling materials, many fear that the result will be messy or unrefined. This book will show you that a thrifty garden can be a beautiful garden. So, whether you're looking to give your garden a makeover or you're thinking about where to start with the empty or overgrown space outside your doors, the thriftier gardening approach is better for both the environment and your purse.

A garden should be alive with wildlife and the easiest way to foster a buzzing environment for very little money is to create the right wildlife environments by growing plants rich in nectar and pollen. Of course I rely on trusted stalwarts, but I also like to try plants I've never grown.

Above Rather than going to landfill, plastic crates can be used to grow squashes and pumpkins.

So, for added drama or excitement, I rely on plants that just get on with it, with little maintenance or human intervention, and which don't cost the earth. The joy and excitement of discovering these new plants and seeing them thrive in your garden is unparalleled, and I'd encourage every gardener to try it.

Be less wasteful

In this book, I'll share my innovative ways for you to save money, enjoy gardening without it becoming a chore and demonstrate how nature can give you a helping hand, whether you're a first-time gardener, a community gardener, allotmenteer or want to find out how to work with a rented outdoor space.

If you're interested in growing ornamentals (flowers, shrubs or trees) or edibles (vegetables, herbs, fruit and edimentals – plants that are both edible and ornamental), rest assured there are simple, low-cost techniques you can introduce to improve your outdoor space. Look at your garden as a living eco-garden that is self-sustainable by reducing the need for water and energy. Attract wildlife with the right plants. Be less wasteful and still have a productive garden by introducing a range of plants that can be grown from seeds, cuttings or division.

Consider recycling as a positive thing and use recycled and upcycled materials sourced from local charity stores, skips, flea markets, car boot sales, salvage and reclamation yards, as well as from friends, family or neighbours. This is the backbone to saving money, using it wisely and being less wasteful. And, by selecting native plants or their cultivated cousins, you'll give your garden a sense of place – one that fits within the local environment.

Buy for the long term

Whether starting from scratch or pondering how to tackle an existing garden, observation is key: take your time and look at your garden a bit differently. Little changes can have a large impact; planning and working in small areas will be key to success. While we all dream of a gorgeous, immaculate garden filled with plants, this takes time. You should work outwards from the house, and while some skill with hammer, drill and saw will go a long way, you will not need to be a pro DIYer. Expect your garden to change over time as your needs change. By making an investment in your garden early on, you can reduce the need to replace things later on. I always say buy the best quality you can afford. For paving, furniture, ornamentation and lighting, consider materials with built-in longevity, such as metal, hardwoods, glass, composite decking and cladding, as well as natural materials. Where possible, choose water-repellent materials for soft furnishings and removable, washable covers so you can replace just the foam cushions inside. If recycled fabric isn't weatherproof, you can make a waterproof solution from white spirit and clear calking for very little money. Gardens need time to grow, as do you as a gardener. Not having cash at the start might be an obstacle, but this will allow you to take your time. Spending wisely on plants and materials up front will benefit you in the future.

I love gardens and gardening as they do not discriminate on age, sex, sexual preference or disability – gardening is for everyone. If you follow my steps, tricks, handy tips and inspiring ideas, you'll have the confidence to grow your own food (reducing your food bill) or healthy, happy ornamentals that will give you years of enjoyment.

Work with nature

When we think of a garden, we often envision a carefully curated space filled with aesthetically pleasing plants, perhaps a well-placed table and chairs, some garden sculpture or a water feature; however, these elements can be expensive.

Many gardeners now view gardens not just as decorative spaces but as living ecosystems and I urge you all to do the same. This recognizes the interconnectedness of all living organisms and their vital role in creating a sustainable, harmonious environment. You have the power to shape your garden into a sustainable haven for biodiversity. By planting to encourage more diversity, you'll attract more wildlife, which will act as natural pest controls, also saving you money.

The ideal thrifty garden will be beautiful to look at and sit in, include water butts to collect free rain, bug hotels and natural habitats to invite in the wildlife, have mixed planting to attract a wide-range of pollinators and other beneficial insects, hedging for birds to nest in, trees for shelter and wildlife, and have compost bins – the natural recycler. It should also include somewhere to sit and relax, pathways from A to B, and somewhere to store your gardening items, perhaps a shed where you can also shelter from harsh weather and sow seeds and pot up plants.

Avoiding synthetic fertilizers and pesticides in favour of organic alternatives you can make from plants and household items you already own is safer for the environment, wildlife and you. Organic gardening supports soil health, encourages beneficial microorganisms and reduces the risk of harmful chemical residues affecting wildlife and water sources. In a garden with a balance of predators and prey, natural pest control can occur, reducing the reliance on harmful chemicals and saving you money.

Creating a flourishing, self-sustaining ecosystem that works with nature is satisfying and isn't hard. Witnessing the dynamic interactions of the seasons, the weather, soil microorganisms, plants, insects and animals in perfect harmony is an extremely gratifying experience; one that cements your connection with nature.

Opposite A simple metal bucket makes the perfect mini-pond for wildlife.

Take it slow

When starting with a new garden or transforming an existing one, take your time and don't be tempted to rush in. The first year will be about understanding your outdoor space, preparing the garden, observing and working on small areas and gradually working outwards. I appreciate that first-time or novice gardeners might find the observational stages tricky to understand. The mindful act of simply appreciating your garden, sitting in it, watching what's happening, and making notes as you're present in the moment will help you get to know your garden as your observations add to your knowledge and experience. Plants might take a while to get going, homemade compost might turn out a bit dry or too wet the first time, or selected materials and plants might not work. But, it's ok for things to take time. It might take years for the border or container to flourish the way you imagined it or be self-sustaining and completely eco-friendly. The wonderful thing about thrifty gardening is that you can take your time and be choosy regarding what seeds or plants you want to add. Focusing on smaller areas, rather than attempting to complete the whole garden in a single year, will help save you money and be less wasteful. The only differences between a gardener who has been doing it for years and a first-time gardener are: time, experience, how much has been learned from their mistakes, and how well they know their garden.

Below Old tyres have been repurposed as containers for these buxus plants at The Breaker's Yard, London.

How to use this book

There is no need to read this book from cover to cover. It is divided into manageable sections you can dip into as you need them.

I'll help navigate you through getting your garden ready, by understanding and reading your garden, looking at aspect, wind direction, gardening styles and more. We'll also delve into what is meant by biodiversity, ecology, sustainability, permaculture, organic gardening, regenerative cover crops, homemade composting and mulches. Soil is key in any garden, so I'll explain the different soil types, how to test your soil and why it should be tested in not just one spot of your garden. And, of course, I'll be sharing tips and tools on how to save money and be generally thriftier in the garden. The main chapters are as follows:

Understanding and planning your garden

Planning your garden will look at certain recycling elements that can make all the difference to your everyday gardening jobs and budgets, as well as the practical considerations you need to think about before putting your design onto paper. Budget, of course, will be a major factor. Still, with the help of task tables and step-by-step approaches, you will soon learn what you can do yourself and when it may be more cost-effective to commission a garden designer or contractor to undertake some of the work. We shall also look at planning the layout, including hedges, walls and barriers, pathways to get you from A to B and the different types of containers and pots you can use in your garden. Finally, we'll look at the finishing touches, such as water features, lighting, furniture and privacy, whether you have a large garden or a small space.

Choosing your plants

Next is the exciting stage of creating your garden, where we'll look at the seasons, successional planting, shape, colour, form, texture, scent, layers and general border designs. In my opinion, a garden should be alive with wildlife, so I'll guide you on how to work with wildlife before we focus on the main stars of the show – the plants! From ornamental bulbs to trees and everything in between and delicious and nutritious edibles, such as vegetables, fruits, edimentals and herbs.

Caring for your garden

The final section focuses on caring for your garden. There is no such thing as a no-maintenance plant, but by selecting the right plants for your lifestyle, you can create and care for low-maintenance plants. And by choosing the right mix of plants for sustainability, biodiversity and ecology, you can have a thriving garden from which you can propogate, and I'll share with you the top take-home ideas and tips so that you can make more plants for free, whether it's from seeds, stem cuttings or division.

To round off the book, I'll share key seasonal gardening jobs so you can sit back and enjoy your new thriftier garden.

UNDERSTANDING YOUR GARDEN

Before you even step outside and start digging, it's essential to have a plan. And, to pull together a working plan, you need to understand some essential gardening ideas. By learning more about gardening, you'll gain the confidence to do more, which, in turn, will save you money. Now, I'm not suggesting that you study horticulture, but understanding key gardening ideas, terminology and practices will help you make informed decisions so that your thrifty garden remains a self-sustaining ecosystem. This chapter will help you get started.

Getting to grips with these gardening ideas will help you choose the right plants, which you can then use to propagate new plants for free and which will, in turn, thrive in your garden. And, the process of getting to know your garden and working out what makes a thrifty garden is free!

There are four key considerations, all explained further in the book: the temperature; soil type; wind; and how much sun and shade there is. By choosing the right plants well-suited to these specific growing conditions, you'll save money as the plants will not wither and die. With your overall plan to hand, select plants with similar water requirements and arrange them together. This allows for efficient irrigation practices, ensuring each plant receives just the right amount of water. Finally, applying a layer of mulch around plants will retain soil moisture, suppress weeds and regulate soil temperature; it can also add a decorative element.

Go around your neighbourhood and nearby countryside and see what's growing in your surroundings, including other people's gardens. Being a little nosey will help you determine what plants thrive in your neighbourhood. Choose native plants, or their cultivated cousins, as they have evolved to thrive in the local conditions. Remember to select a mix of plants that provide interest throughout the seasons, including those with attractive foliage, flowers, seedheads or berries. This ensures that your thrifty garden remains visually appealing year-round. Lastly, remember that you'll need to monitor your garden regularly for signs of stress.

The big picture

A thrifty gardener must look at the larger picture before settling on the details. Think holistically and seek to cultivate plants, conserve resources and promote long-term wellbeing for you, the gardener, garden and the surrounding ecosystem. We are environmental stewards of our gardens.

When sourcing materials, choose seasonal and locally available items, which can be both sustainable and cost-effective. Locally sourced compost, mulch, plants, paving, gravel and timber will have a lower environmental impact, as will hunting for recycled materials from skips, sheds, car boot sales, flea markets, friends and family.

Be resilient

The thrifty garden must become resilient to a changing climate. A climate-smart approach to thrifty gardening involves thoughtful consideration of various environmental factors, such as understanding wind patterns, creating microclimates using shrubs and trees and embracing seasonal variations. By doing so, you can create a thrifty garden that helps plant health, conserves water and contributes to overall ecological resilience.

Biodiversity, short for biological diversity, refers to a variety of living organisms – both plant and animal – within a particular ecosystem such as your garden, and is essential for the health and stability of your garden. But why does diverse plant selection matter? In short, it ensures that a garden is better equipped to handle fluctuations in temperature, precipitation and extreme weather events. This diversity acts as a natural buffer against the unpredictability of climate change.

Growing different plant species will help disrupt the lifecycle of pests and diseases. If you were to grow just a single plant species, known as monoculture, your garden would be more susceptible to the rapid spread of pests. By adding a diverse planting mix, you'll not only help promote natural pest control, but it will also contribute to the aesthetic appeal of your garden. Different colours, shapes and textures create visually engaging gardens. While diverse plant selection is vital, challenges do exist. You will need to be mindful of your plant choices to, for example, avoid introducing species that may become invasive, thereby threatening biodiversity.

Try native plants

Selecting native plants aligns your garden with the region's natural flora. Native plants have evolved alongside local wildlife, providing essential food sources and habitats. Native and climate-adapted plants often require less water than exotic species. This is particularly critical in regions facing water scarcity and drought conditions. Over the last few years, we have seen extreme weather patterns across the globe.

Above Resilient native plants, such as poppies, cornflowers and oxeye daisies can be grown in the poorest soil, adding colour and benefitting a range of pollinators.

A biodiverse mix of plants that have evolved in specific climates is better equipped to handle the extremes associated with climate change, including heatwaves, storms, floods and erratic rainfall. These native plants are valuable assets in the creation of your thrifty climate-resilient garden because they have developed several forms of adaptive resilience, such as:

+ deep root systems that enable plants to tap into water reserves deep in the soil
+ modified leaf structures that minimize water loss through transpiration, such as light-reflecting leaf surfaces
+ flexible stems that can bend with the wind
+ root structures that enhance oxygen uptake, while others exhibit a capacity for rapid growth following floods, allowing them to recover swiftly.

This also means that if one species faces challenges, others may thrive.

Good, healthy soil is important in any garden, but especially in thrifty gardens. The good news is that native plants contribute to soil health and carbon sequestration. Their root systems enhance soil structure, preventing erosion during storms and sequester carbon through organic matter accumulation, such as homemade compost, well-rotted manure and organic mulches. A thriving soil ecosystem is rich in biodiversity, including beneficial microorganisms, insects and other soil-dwelling organisms. This biodiversity helps support your plants' health, enhances natural pest control and contributes to the overall resilience of the garden ecosystem.

Go organic

I garden organically, and I urge all gardeners to do the same. Back in the 1970s, my grandfather taught me the importance of good, healthy soil, something quite rare when pesticides and herbicides were being used frequently and everywhere. Organic gardening is simple: you prioritize natural and sustainable methods while minimizing synthetic chemicals and fertilizers. Thrifty gardeners will find organic gardening a cost-effective and environmentally friendly way to create a flourishing garden.

Healthy soil is the building block of organic gardening. If your soil is not great, add soil conditioners, such as well-rotted manure or homemade compost. Once you have healthy soil, your plants will need companion plants which have natural affinities with each other. Planting them together can help deter pests, improve pollination and maximize space. Around the plants, mulch the soil with homemade compost, grass clippings or by re-purposing cardboard boxes, which helps retain soil moisture, reduces evaporation and suppresses weeds. Then, later in the year, you can collect seeds, preserve and replant seeds from your harvest. This thrifty practice reduces the need to purchase new seeds each season and helps maintain plant varieties adapted to your garden.

Savour water

Water is an essential resource in any garden, yet its scarcity and the environmental challenges we face today make it increasingly important to conserve and manage this precious asset wisely. Overwatering can lead to soil degradation, including compaction and erosion. When water is not absorbed properly by the soil, it often runs off, taking with it valuable topsoil and nutrients. This run-off can also contribute to water pollution, carrying fertilizers, pesticides and other chemicals into nearby bodies of water.

A garden designed to conserve water often focuses on improving soil health, essential for plant growth. Healthy soil with good structure can retain moisture for longer, reducing the need for frequent watering. Techniques such as mulching, incorporating organic matter and choosing appropriate plant species can enhance the soil's ability to hold water while allowing roots to access it more efficiently.

Top A wooden barrel can easily be connected to a downpipe to make a water butt.

Above An old bath is the perfect dunking station - just remember to plug the flow.

Savouring water in your garden is not just about using less; it's about using it wisely. By watering plants in a controlled and thoughtful manner, rather than overwatering, we encourage deep root growth. Certain watering techniques, such as drip irrigation and watering early in the morning or late in the evening, reduce evaporation and ensure that water is directed precisely where it's needed. And, by grouping plants according to their water needs, you can avoid overwatering or underwatering individual plants.

Collecting rainwater in barrels, water butts and recycled water barrels provides a free source of water that can be used during dry periods. Permeable surfaces, such as gravel, bark or stone chippings, will help direct water to plant beds. Water features, such as ponds with a mix of aquatic plant life, can help influence the microclimate of your garden. Evaporation from water surfaces can cool the surrounding air, creating a more favourable environment for plants and reducing the overall temperature. And water, whether in the form of a bird bath made from an upturned bin lid, reflective pool in an upcycled metal container or natural pond, will attract a wide range of wildlife. Birds, insects and amphibians are drawn to water sources, creating a balanced ecosystem where natural predators help control pests. So, not only can you give your plants the right amount of water, you can attract wildlife to care for them - working with nature to save you money!

Invite wildlife

Wildlife-friendly, thrifty gardening goes beyond mere aesthetics; it's a conscientious effort to create spaces that support local flora and fauna. Planting nectar-rich flowers, providing habitat features such as birdhouses and insect hotels made from gravel boards or recycled floorboards, and avoiding harmful pesticides will enhance biodiversity and foster ecological resilience. Nectar-rich flowers serve as vital food sources for pollinators such as bees, butterflies and birds, and a diverse array of such plants ensures a continuous supply of nectar throughout the growing season. Selecting plants with different bloom times and flower shapes accommodates many pollinators. Hybridized plants (the resulting plant from a cross between two different species or varieties) may lack the nectar or pollen content necessary for the sustenance of pollinators, but choosing heirloom or non-hybridized varieties ensures that plants retain their natural characteristics, providing valuable resources for wildlife. By inviting wildlife into your garden, you introduce natural predators, which, in turn, will help keep down pests and therefore reduce the need for shop-bought pesticides, which can also be harmful to wildlife and the environment.

Above Broken garden items, such as terracotta pots and pieces of wood, can be layered with palettes to house wildlife.

Repurpose and recycle

Gardens are the best place to think of recycling. And to be clear, recycling here will cover everything, including 'upcycling', 'repurposing' and 'reusing'. I was told from a young age to recycle as much as possible, make the most of what we had and make it our own. Fortunately, there are so many ways to recycle things to create beautiful gardens. And, as we know, gardening can be an expensive pastime, if you let it, so if we can save money and reinvest it into other things for our outdoor spaces then we balance the 'gardening cost scales'.

Recycling can be approached from an aesthetics point of view – that is, how something looks or is designed to give a cohesive feel to your garden that you're happy with – and a practical one. When we think of the latter, we automatically think of saving money or re-purposing an object as something else that we might not have, but having local material to hand when you need it also saves time. If you think a garden full of recycled objects will not fit your aesthetic, then use the material(s) for items that will not be on show all the time, such as wooden seed trays or small containers used for propagation. Alternatively, think ahead and see how a rampant climbing plant might obscure a recycled object. A lot goes on in the garden that we don't see regularly. A productive area of the garden with a cold frame and raised beds made from recycled materials can be screened off, and, if you're a handy DIYer, then closely inspect mass-produced items, such as wooden screening, and repurpose your recycled materials to match.

If, like so many, you like using an object as a substitute for something else, then this approach and book is for you. Although most of these ideas can be used in any garden, they work well in small spaces where a range of plants, from tasty fruits and nourishing veggies to flowering plants, trees and shrubs, can be successfully grown in recycled containers and tighter spots – you need less space than you may think.

Above Hardcore from the site has been repurposed to form retaining edges to the borders and to create mini walls.

Opposite An old rusty wheel has been filled with a gritty mix, perfect for succulents, while scaffold boards form raised beds.

Lack of funds need not be a barrier to building and creating your garden if you repurpose and recycle materials. You may not need to buy expensive items if you look around your neighbourhood to see if there are skips full of building material or items that can be repurposed, and ask friends, family members, neighbours and community groups if they are getting rid of anything.

It's also wise to steer away from bold statements and gardening trends, as changing fashions can be expensive. Keep things simple and have an overall plan. You can paint recycled object(s) to match existing features and each other to create a cohesive feel and look.

OLIVE
KALAMATA
eccelenti

Grow your own

Growing your own food is a thrifty, sustainable choice that offers benefits beyond the simple reduction in grocery bills. Cultivating edible plants at home provides fresh, high-quality produce that you might otherwise have to buy at a premium, and you get control over how it's grown, ensuring it's organic and free from chemicals. Additionally, many edible plants are also ornamental, helping you to create a beautiful and functional garden.

Enhance garden aesthetics

Incorporating edibles such as rainbow chard, kale and nasturtiums alongside ornamental plants enhances garden aesthetics, as these plants come in a range of colours, textures and forms. They add visual interest and can even attract pollinators, supporting overall garden health. For instance, purple cabbages and trailing strawberries bring a pop of colour and variety to beds and borders, while herbs like thyme and rosemary add a subtle, attractive greenery. This approach creates a harmonious balance between decorative and practical, productive plants, making your garden a beautiful, thriving ecosystem.

Multiply your harvest

One of the most economical and surprising ways to start a food garden is by using produce bought at the supermarket. Many kitchen scraps and leftovers can be grown into full plants with minimal effort, reducing waste and eliminating the need to buy seeds or seedlings. Spring onions, for example, will regrow if placed in water, and cuttings from herbs like basil and coriander will root in water, giving you a fresh supply at no additional cost. Garlic cloves, potatoes and even celery bases can be planted directly into the soil and will grow into full plants, stretching what was initially a single grocery item into multiple harvests.

Cut down costs

Growing food from supermarket produce is an easy way to experiment with new varieties while cutting down on the costs associated with growing from seed or buying established plants. For example, tomatoes and peppers often contain seeds that can be saved, dried and sown, allowing you to cultivate your own plants without needing to buy new ones. While not all supermarket produce will be suited for home growing – some items may be treated to prevent sprouting – many will flourish, especially if chosen from organic sections.

Towards self-sufficiency

Overall, growing your own at home, especially by creatively repurposing supermarket items, is a wise and rewarding way to save money while adding a functional beauty to your garden. You're not only reducing grocery expenses but also taking steps towards self-sufficiency, growing food right at your doorstep. As the garden matures, the satisfaction of eating produce you've nurtured yourself adds a deeper layer of connection to nature and food.

Getting to know your garden

One of the first steps to getting to know your garden is to work out what you want your garden to do for you and then how much you intend to spend on it. Being frugal can be a way of life and gardening can be one of the thriftiest hobbies and you'll still reap huge rewards, whether through edibles or ornamentals. For you to do it well and for it to be successful, you need to enjoy gardening. What you do in your garden, and how thrifty you can be, can therefore impact your life, so understanding the intricacies of your outdoor space, considering factors such as microclimates and soil composition are paramount.

Your microclimate

Your garden is not a uniform environment; it consists of microclimates created by variations in sunlight, wind exposure, humidity, temperature and barriers, such as hedges, shrubs, trees, fences and walls. To get an idea of the microclimates in your garden, draw a rough sketch of it from a bird's eye view. This is known as a plan view. On the drawing, note:

+ the aspect, i.e. does the garden face north, east, south or west. This can sometimes be confusing, especially if your garden is long or large since areas further away from the house might face, or receive sunlight from, a different direction to those closer to it
+ areas that receive full sun, partial shade or full shade throughout the day
+ where the prevailing wind comes from.

This exercise is a great excuse to sit in a garden chair all day to observe where the sun and shadows fall. Understanding these microclimates allows you to strategically place plants where they can flourish, matching their sunlight and water requirements to the garden's natural conditions. If you have a sunny spot near a wall, for example, it can create a warm microclimate perfect for sun-loving plants like lavender, tomatoes or peppers, while shadier areas are ideal for ferns or hostas. Also consider the position of any mature trees in your garden, or any new trees that you are considering adding, as these will create their own microclimate. Trees can cool their surroundings through a process called transpiration, when water absorbed through their roots releases as water vapour through tiny openings in their leaves called stomata. By blocking out light, trees can reduce soil surface temperatures, they can increase humidity levels and cool soil temperatures.

The lie of the land

Pay attention to the contours of your garden. Identify low-lying areas where water might accumulate and spots where drainage is efficient. Proper drainage is vital to prevent waterlogged soil, which can lead to root rot and other plant diseases. By understanding the topography (the lie of the land), you can plan the layout of your garden to optimize water flow and prevent potential issues. If a low-lying area is prone to water accumulation, consider planting moisture-tolerant species like irises or ferns, rather than spending money on trying to alter the terrain; however, raised beds or strategic grading of soil can help improve drainage.

Planters made from soft- or hardwood sleepers, recycled wood, pallets or corrugated roofing filled with soil make great raised beds. Note, however, that filling a raised bed with purchased soil will be costly. Soil from elsewhere in the garden if you have it is fine, for example if you're planning a pond to attract wildlife. For the top 15cm (6in) of soil use either homemade or bought compost (buying it will be inevitable in the first year or so). After a couple of years, your homemade compost will suffice for the entire raised bed. Add a layer of cardboard at the bottom before you fill it to prevent any ground weeds from growing up through your raised bed. Use water butts to collect water from downpipes, repurposing rainwater for your garden and taking it away from the soil's surface during heavy rain. This reduces water bills and ensures a sustainable water source for your plants, which is better than tap water. If you have an area of the garden that gets sodden during heavy rains, then consider adding a rain garden, with plants that are suited to wetter conditions. These will help soak up excess water and keep run-off to a minimum.

Top/Above Gardens are never flat. Follow the contours of the land rather than spending a fortune on adding terracing or retaining walls.

Wind

Take note of any prevailing winds. If it's a still day when looking out at your garden, you might be able to tell where the wind comes from by looking at your or neighbours' trees. If they are leaning in one direction or are misshapen this will reveal where the wind comes from. If you live near the sea, then you'll need to deal with salt-laden winds and therefore your choice of plants will need to take this into account, such as rosemary, cordyline and achillea.

Wind can significantly impact your garden, affecting both plants and structures. Identifying prevailing wind directions will help influence the growth of your plants. Understanding wind patterns helps you create a garden that is resilient to the elements. If your garden is exposed to strong winds, for example, grow windbreaks using tall, sturdy plants like trees and shrubs. A mix of evergreen and deciduous shrubs and trees works better throughout the year. These can shield more delicate plants from wind damage. Alternatively, fences, trellises and walls made from recycled materials can also serve as effective windbreaks.

For the thrifty gardener, creating a living screen using bare-root hedging is far cheaper and more sustainable than building a wall or erecting a fence. Open trellises can be built from roofing lathes, bamboo canes or broken-up pallets. Just be mindful, however, of the wind shelter on the other side of the prevailing wind. As wind hits a windbreak, it's forced up and over it onto the other side. This excess wind could affect plants in borders or pots further away from the windbreak. This is why windbreaks with an open structure, such as slatted fencing and trellis, as well as hedging, work better than a solid structure, as the wind is filtered through the gaps, reducing its speed as it goes through.

Wind can also be seen as a positive for the thrifty gardener. Pruning shrubs and trees with an open structure will allow wind to pass through, which can help keep pests and diseases at bay.

Above A simple windbreak trellis made from bamboo canes, covered in foliage, filters out the wind, slowing it down.

Take stock

If you've moved to a new house with a garden full of plants, or you want to start a new garden, it's essential to take stock of the plants already thriving in your garden. Plant identification apps on mobile phones, such as PlantSnap, Fryd, and PIcture This, help with this. Also, look around beyond your garden at local parks, neighbours' gardens, and the countryside or community gardens. Look out for native plants, as these are often well-adapted to the local environment, typically requiring less maintenance and contributing to the overall biodiversity of your garden. This is tricky, but with time and searching online or in books you'll start to build a picture of the native plants in your area. Incorporate native plants or their cultivated cousins into your garden. Also, observe which plants attract pollinators and beneficial insects, as this will provide insights into creating a balanced and thriving ecosystem. Many native plants can be grown from seed – look online for seed companies, or if it's possible to collect them, do so, but always get permission from the land owner before taking seeds from plants.

Observation and recording is key when it comes to identifying native plants. If you're new to gardening, spotting a native plant will be tricky. Taking photos on your phone will help you search for them online. You may also find multiple sites in your area having the same plants, which could be an indication that it's a native plant. But rest assured, over time, as you learn more about plants, you'll be able to spot them, note their characteristics and work them seamlessly into your planting schemes.

Below An established garden may be overwhelming, but don't be scared of moving around the plants you want to keep.

Feel the soil

Gardening is a tactile pastime and getting your bare hands into soil releases serotonin, the feel-good chemical, in the brain. Knowing what soil you have is essential for healthy, happy garden plants. Healthy soil needs to contain nitrogen, potassium and phosphorous. Nitrogen is probably the most beneficial nutrient for plants' healthy green colour and energy to grow and produce flowers and fruit. Potassium helps with photosynthesis and the development of flowers and fruit. While phosphorous works under the soil for healthy root development while also contributing to fruits, flowers and seeds, it also contributes to fighting disease.

Soil pH

Conduct a soil test to determine your soil's pH level and nutrient composition. Knowing this is invaluable for selecting plants that will thrive in those specific soil conditions, reducing the need for expensive soil amendments. It also means that you'll not waste money on plants as they fail under the wrong growing conditions. Every inch of soil in your garden tells a story and that's why it's important to do several soil tests around your garden.

Above Good old bicarbonate of soda added to moistened soil starts a fizzing reaction, an indication of acidic soil.

+ A pH of 7 is considered neutral.
+ Anything below 7 is acidic.
+ Anything above 7 is considered alkaline.

If your soil is acidic, consider azaleas and blueberries. For alkaline soil, opt for lavender or yarrow. You can use these homemade recipes with bicarbonate of soda or vinegar to determine your soil's pH:

Put 2 tbsp of soil into a glass and moisten with distilled water. Add 8 tbsp of bicarbonate of soda. If it fizzes then the soil is acidic.

Repeat the process with a fresh batch of soil and add 8 tbsp of vinegar. If it fizzes then the soil is alkaline. If neither of these show any fizzing then the soil is neutral.

Top to bottom Clay soil can be formed into a ball. Sandy soil breaks apart. Clay loam is a crumbly mix. Chalk soil is seen as the worst type.

Soil texture

Colour can give insights into the type of soil you have. Blackish-brown soil is associated with concentrations of organic matter, while red or yellow soils indicate minerals such as aluminium and iron, as well as clay and moderate moisture levels. Grey soils are normally found in wetlands high in iron or sulphur and light-coloured soils, white to light grey, are found in coastal areas.

There are six main types of soil:

1. Clay
2. Sand
3. Silt
4. Peat
5. Chalk
6. Loam.

Many gardeners consider chalk soil as the worst type of soil, because it's free-draining and contains a lot of lime, which restricts the range of plants that you can grow. Loam soil is the soil of most gardeners' dreams: a mix of organic matter, free-draining particles and the ability to hold on to water and nutrients. With work, over several years, all soils can become loam soil.

Take a handful of damp soil and squeeze it.

+ Sandy soil feels gritty and falls easily between your fingers.
+ Clay soil feels sticky and holds its shape when rolled into a ball.
+ Loam soil has a balanced, crumbly texture that smears then breaks up.

Collect soil samples, add water and shake them in a jam jar. Over time, the particles settle, helping you observe the layers and determine the proportion of sand, silt and clay. Observe how water drains in your garden. Fast drainage may indicate sandy soil, while slow drainage may suggest clay soil.

New-build soil

In the garden of a newly built house, you're likely to dig up lots of rubble, broken glass and other detritus left by the builders. The soil will also be compacted from heavy foot traffic and machinery. The thrifty gardener can change this and even find the waste rubble positively useful. Insert a garden fork into the soil and wiggle it back and forth to loosen the soil and then, if possible, start to turn the soil. Remove the rubble and pile it to one side as it can be used at the bottom of raised beds to aid drainage or be crushed up to form a sub-base for low walls or paved areas. You'll be gardening on subsoil. By adding organic matter over the years and getting soil-borne microorganisms to work for you, the organic matter starts to break down (and become humus), which can be added into the soil to make loam. This crumbly topsoil is then ideal for growing a wide range of plants, such as root vegetables, leafy greens, herbs, fruit trees, shrubs and herbaceous perennials. But don't worry, there are numerous resilient plants that will grow in the poor soil until the soil has been improved, namely, carrots, beans, herbs, echinacea, coreopsis, cotoneaster, forsythia and hawthorn.

Improve your soil

Thrifty gardeners can improve any soil type by adding organic matter. Homemade compost, well-rotted manure and leaf mould all enhance soil structure, fertility and water retention, creating a healthier and more productive garden. Spread the organic matter over the soil's surface in autumn and spring and gently work it in with a garden fork. You can also use it as a mulch to prevent water evaporation and suppress weeds. Good soil structure allows for air and water movement, creating the right environment for root growth. Compacted soil restricts root growth, so aerating soil is key by spiking or coring (removing small plugs of soil) and by adding organic matter.

Top Use broken bricks and stones as a mulch or as a border edging material. **Above** Compost from seasonal displays can be added as a mulch.

Making your own compost is critical for saving money, reducing reliance on commercial additives and enriching your garden soil. It is a fantastic way to recycle organic waste, such as kitchen scraps (but no dairy or meat), garden clippings, annual weeds and prunings. Composting, a natural process involving decomposing organic materials by microorganisms, reduces waste and creates a nutrient-rich soil amendment that can improve plant health and structure. The result is a dark, crumbly substance known as compost.

Successful composting

A mix of brown and green organic material at the right ratios is needed for the best compost.

1. **Carbon-rich materials (browns)** these include dry leaves, straw, cardboard and sawdust. They provide energy for the microorganisms.

2. **Nitrogen-rich materials (greens)** these include kitchen scraps (fruit and vegetable peels), grass clippings, coffee grounds and manure. They supply the microorganisms with protein.

3. **Moisture** the compost pile needs to be kept moist, about as wet as a wrung-out sponge.

4. **Air** turning the compost pile regularly introduces oxygen, which is crucial for aerobic decomposition.

You can build a simple bin using old wood or chicken wire. Ensure it has good ventilation and easy access for turning. The optimum compost bin size is 1m × 1m × 1m (approximately 3ft × 3ft × 3ft), so recycled wooden pallets, readily available and cheap, are perfect. If you have space, you can create an open compost pile. Choose a location with good drainage and partial shade to keep the pile from drying out too quickly. Chicken wire and some wooden posts or thick prunings can help keep the pile in a single location.

What to include

+ Kitchen scraps: eggshells, coffee grounds, tea bags, vegetable peelings
+ Garden waste: grass clippings, spent potting compost, shredded branches, stems and twigs, cut perennial stems
+ Annual weeds
+ Manure
+ Cardboard and paper, shredded
+ Straw and hay

What not to include

- Meat, dairy, grease or whole eggs, as these will attract vermin
- Heavily printed magazines
- Perennial weeds
- Pet faeces, spent cat litter
- Thick cardboard
- Diseased plant material

Above Collecting your cuttings in a bucket is a simple way to ensure you keep them chopped up, perfect for adding to the compost.
Opposite Deciduous leaves can be added to the compost heap or made into leaf mould.

A good compost

Every gardener will have their own compost mix, but if in doubt aim for a ratio of 70:30 brown to green organic material. As the material decomposes, microorganisms, such as beneficial bacteria, fungi, actinomycetes (bacteria that break down tougher organic materials), protozoa and nematodes (microscopic creatures that feed on bacteria and fungi) get to work to further break down the material. The end result should be a crumbly, dark and earthy-smelling material, rich in nutrients, perfect for enriching your soil.

Composting can feel daunting at first, and it's easy to become disheartened if the results aren't what you expect. But like gardening itself, composting is a process of learning, experimenting and observing nature at work. Early attempts often go wrong because of simple things like too much kitchen waste, not enough dry material, or forgetting to turn the pile. These are not failures, but lessons in balance. Composting is essentially nature's recycling system, and it will always try to right itself over time. Even if your first heap turns slimy, smelly or dry, it can be revived with a few adjustments. With patience, practise and a willingness to adapt, you'll soon create rich, crumbly compost – one of the most rewarding contributions you can make to your soil.

Ingredients

Carbon-rich materials (browns)

+ 2 parts dry leaves
+ 1 part shredded newspaper or cardboard
+ 1 part straw or sawdust

Nitrogen-rich materials (greens)

+ 1 part vegetable and fruit scraps
+ 1 part grass clippings
+ 1 part coffee grounds

Optional additions

+ Eggshells (for calcium)
+ Seaweed or algae (for trace minerals)
+ Manure from herbivores (chickens, horses, cows)

1.

Layering: start with a layer of coarse materials (like small branches or straw) to promote airflow at the bottom. Alternate with layers of all the other ingredients listed, in layers of browns and greens, aiming for a ratio of 70:30 brown to greens.

2.

Moisture: ensure each layer is moist but not soggy.

3.

Turning: turn the pile with a garden fork or compost aerator every 1–2 weeks. This introduces oxygen and speeds up the decomposition process.

4.

Monitor: the compost pile should heat up as microorganisms break down the materials. If it's too dry, add water; if too wet, add more browns.

Above Grass clippings, shredded paper, eggshells and water in the right mix make the perfect compost.

Hot compost

Hot composting is a method of composting that speeds up the decomposition process by creating optimal conditions for heat-loving microorganisms to thrive. Carefully manage the compost pile to maintain high temperatures, typically between 55 and 71°C (130 and 160°F), by turning the pile of materials regularly to allow air into the mix. Organic materials break down more quickly at these temperatures, resulting in finished compost in a few weeks to a few months, rather than the several months or even years it can take with cold composting. Additional benefits include pathogen and weed-seed destruction and efficient nutrient recycling.

Ingredients

+ 1 part grass clippings (fresh and moist – don't add too much as it can make the compost soggy)
+ 1 part fruit and vegetable scraps
+ 1 part dried leaves
+ 1 part shredded paper/cardboard
+ 1 handful of a compost activator, such as fish, blood and bone meal or seaweed

1.
Mix thoroughly: combine the ingredients and mix them well.

2.
Build the pile: aim for a pile size of at least 90cm (around 3ft) in all dimensions. Larger piles retain heat better.

3.
Turn regularly: turn the pile every 2–3 days to maintain high temperatures.

Troubleshooting

Odour
If your compost smells bad, it might be too wet or lack sufficient airflow. Turn the pile and add more browns.

Pests
Fruit flies or rodents can be a problem. Ensure you're not adding meat or dairy and turn the pile frequently.

Slow decomposition
If your compost decomposes slowly, it might need more nitrogen-rich materials or better aeration.

Harvesting compost

Not making your own compost is wasteful of money and a natural resource. Good compost takes time to make. It's good practice to turn your compost heap regularly, so that the drier material on the edges gets incorporated into the heated centre. If you have the space, then two or three bins are perfect, as you can tip and empty one bin into the next until it has all rotted down. I've used both solid-sided and slatted compost bins and prefer the latter as it allows for good airflow. Compost can take 3–6 months to be ready, depending on the method and conditions.

To harvest

1.

Use a sieve to separate finished compost from any undecomposed materials. Return the undecomposed bits to the pile or use these for mulching pots, containers and borders.

2.

Apply compost to your garden beds, mix it into the soil or use it as a top dressing for plants.

Tips for successful composting

Balance and chopping
Maintain the right balance of browns and greens and cut or shred larger materials to speed up decomposition.

Size matters
Larger piles decompose faster due to better insulation and heat retention.

Monitor temperature
A well-maintained compost pile will be warm, 55–63°C (130–145°F) in the centre. If it cools down, it may need turning or additional nitrogen-rich, green materials.

Turn a new leaf

A simple way of adding structure to your soil is to make your own leaf mould. This is also perfect when used as a growing medium for container-grown plants. In the autumn, collect fallen deciduous leaves, place them in a black bin bag, add a watering can of water, tie up the bag and then make some holes in the bottom for drainage using a garden fork or a knife. Place it somewhere out of sight and leave for 12 months. Alternatively, make an inexpensive leaf bin using four wooden stakes for the corners and wrap some chicken wire all the way around. After a year, you'll have a wonderful crumbly soil conditioner. Alternatives to leaf mould are spent mushroom compost, which helps break up heavy clay soils; cocoa shells, which helps retain moisture in soil; and composted straw, seaweed and composted bark. Composted straw breaks up compacted particles in heavy soils, seaweed is packed with micronutrients and contains growth hormones that promote root growth, while composted bark helps retain moisture and acts as natural weed suppressant when used as a mulch. Each of these soil conditioners has its unique strengths, and they can be combined or used individually depending on your garden's specific needs. By enriching the soil with these organic amendments, you create a healthier environment for plants, leading to stronger growth, more robust yields and a more resilient garden overall.

Above Fill a bin bag with fallen deciduous leaves and add water. This is the start of making leaf mould – a free soil conditioner.

Don't forget to mulch

Mulching is an essential practice for thrifty gardeners, offering numerous benefits to soil health and plant growth with minimal effort and cost. Apply a 5–10cm (2–4in) layer of organic material on top of the soil, such as straw, cardboard, grass or bark chippings or shredded leaves. The mulch helps regulate soil temperature, retain moisture by reducing evaporation and suppress weeds, reducing the need for shop-bought weedkillers.

Allowing the soil to retain water for longer periods is particularly valuable during hot weather or in regions prone to drought. This not only reduces the need for frequent watering but also ensures that plants have a consistent supply of moisture.

By blocking sunlight, mulch prevents weed seeds from germinating, reducing competition for water and nutrients among your plants. Mulching also helps insulate the soil, keeping it cooler in summer and warmer in winter, protecting roots from extreme temperatures.

When organic mulches are used, another key benefit is the gradual improvement of soil fertility and structure. As the mulch breaks down, it adds valuable nutrients to the soil, enhancing its organic matter content. This promotes microbial activity, improving soil aeration and drainage, especially in clay or compacted soils. Moreover, mulch minimizes soil erosion caused by wind and rain, keeping valuable topsoil intact. Covering the soil surface also reduces the risk of soil-borne diseases by preventing splashing during rainfall.

Using cover crops

Cover crops like clover play an important role in sustainable thrifty gardening. For just the cost of some seeds you can soon cover bare soil without the expense of weed-suppressant membrane and pegs or mulching. They improve soil health by adding organic matter, enhancing nutrient content, suppressing weeds and preventing erosion. Clover is a popular choice because it's easy to grow and fixes nitrogen in the soil, making it available for subsequent crops and flowers. The flowers are also ideal for beneficial pollinators. If you're growing your own food, you'd be wise to fill any gaps with quick-growing vegetables, such as carrots, radishes and lettuces, although this is not always possible as sometimes areas need to wait while you're dealing with somewhere else.

Clover can be sown at various times throughout the year, depending on the climate and your goals for the cover crop. Sow in early spring, once the soil is workable, to cover the ground through the growing season. You can also sow in late summer for an autumn cover crop that will overwinter. In mild climates, sowing in late autumn is also an option, as clover can establish itself before the first frost and survive through the winter.

Clover seeds germinate best when the soil temperatures are between 7 and 29°C (45 and 84°F). Temperatures that are cooler or warmer can hinder germination. Selecting the right one from retailers is really important. White clover (*Trifolium repens*) is a perennial variety that spreads well and is good for ground cover. Red clover (*T. pratense*) is a short-lived perennial or biennial that grows taller, making it suitable for cutting and incorporating into the soil as green manure. Crimson clover (*T. incarnatum*) is a quick-growing annual often used as an autumn cover crop to provide a burst of nutrients in spring.

Above Often overlooked, cover crops such as clover can save you money on membrane, pegs and mulch, and is more environmental.

How to sow a cover crop

Start by removing any existing weeds. This prevents competition and ensures that the cover crop establishes itself effectively. Test the soil pH (see page 29) and nutrient levels. Clover prefers a slightly acidic to neutral pH (6.0 to 7.0). If needed, adjust the pH with lime or sulphur. Lightly rake the soil to create a crumbly, fine seedbed, with no large clumps. This helps improve seed-to-soil contact, which is essential for good germination.

Ingredients

+ 200g (7oz) of seed per square metre

1.

Scatter the seeds evenly across the prepared soil. You can do this easily by hand or using a seed spreader for larger areas.

2.

Lightly rake the seeds into the soil or cover them with a thin layer of soil. Clover seeds need light to germinate, so don't bury them too deep – 3–6mm (up to ¼in) is sufficient.

3.

After sowing, water the area gently but thoroughly to ensure good soil-to-seed contact.

4.

Keep the soil consistently moist during the germination period, which typically takes 7 to 15 days. If birds are a concern, you may need to protect the seeded area with twigs and branches until the clover has established.

5.

Once the clover has grown to around 10cm (4in) tall, you can mow it to encourage denser growth and to prevent it overshadowing other plants. Mowing also helps control flowering and seed production if that is not desired.

6.

If you're using clover as green manure, mow it before it flowers and let the cuttings lie on the surface for a few days to wilt slightly. Then, turn them into the soil to add organic matter and nitrogen.

If you plan to overwinter the clover, allow it to grow and protect the soil throughout the winter. In spring, you can mow and incorporate it into the soil as needed. After turning the clover into the soil, give it some time to decompose before planting your main crop. This allows the nutrients to become available to the next plants.

A no-dig approach

Adopting a no-dig or minimum-dig approach means you refrain from turning over the soil with excessive digging. But why is this approach a good idea for the thrifty gardener? Reduced disturbance prevents compaction, allowing for better water infiltration and drainage, which is crucial for plant root health. It also preserves the habitat for soil-dwelling organisms, including beneficial microbes, insects and earthworms, contributing to biodiversity and the eco-friendly approach that is essential for the thrifty gardener.

Use cover crops, mulch or organic matter to suppress weeds instead of relying on extensive soil cultivation. To implement a no-dig approach, you'll first need to clear the area of existing weeds or vegetation, then place a layer of cardboard or several sheets of newspaper over the cleared area. This acts as a barrier to suppress new weeds and encourages earthworms to come to the surface. Apply a thick layer of organic matter on top of the cardboard, then plant directly into the organic matter. Create openings in the mulch in which to place seeds or transplants. The roots will penetrate through the organic layer into the underlying soil. Always maintain a consistent mulch layer and minimize foot traffic to prevent soil compaction.

Below Cover weeded soil with cardboard and a thick layer of organic matter. Ideally, top up with 2–3cm (1–1¼in) of organic matter annually.

Lift your garden with raised beds

Raised beds are an effective way to limit soil disturbance. They can improve drainage, are great for new-build gardens or areas of the garden where the soil is compacted or waterlogged, can prevent soil compaction and provide a controlled environment for plant growth. You can make raised beds from all sorts of salvaged materials.

Raised beds work very well in small spaces, such as gardens and on balconies and rooftops (but be aware they may be very heavy when full and wet). Raised beds don't have to be all the same size or height: consider having taller raised beds at the back and smaller ones in front; this way, you can bring colour up to eye level. Plants in raised beds are easily accessible, but if you're thinking of spaces for wheelchair users, try and avoid flat-sided raised beds as wheelchair user will not be able to get their feet underneath. You can make your own 'raised tables' by constructing a box using the trusty materials mentioned above and securely fixing old table legs to the bottom. You can also add wheels to be able to move beds around your outdoor space.

Top/Below/Opposite Old bricks and railway sleepers make perfect border edging material for edibles and ornamentals.

Seasonal transformations

Your garden will change throughout the seasons and understanding these changes allows you to plan accordingly so that you don't waste money and can provide the right practical solutions and resources. Keep a gardening journal/diary, either digitally or in paper form, making note of how much sun areas of your garden get at different times of the year. Note how sunlight angles change throughout the year and what effect this has on shadows and areas in full sun in your garden. This will help when choosing plants that grow best in full sun, partial or dappled shade or full shade. Temperatures will vary widely from summer to winter, and these fluctuations will impact plant growth. Similarly, heavy rains in winter or spring might lead to waterlogged areas or plant damage. Deciduous trees will lose their leaves in the autumn and these will not return until the spring, offering more light during the winter months.

Hardy plants

Wherever you live, your gardening needs and practices will differ from fellow gardeners who might live in colder areas or those with sunshine and warm temperatures year-round. Knowing and understanding plant hardiness is key to making the right decisions on plant selection and not wasting your money on plants likely to die in your conditions. Hardiness, therefore, refers to temperatures required for plants to thrive and can be broken up into:

+ **Very hardy** (colder than -20°C/-4°F): peony, Siberian iris, blue spruce and dogwood
+ **Hardy** (-15–-5°C/5–23°F): hellebore, Japanese quince, hawthorn and thyme
+ **Half-hardy** (-5–1°C/23–34°F): agapanthus, dahlia, hebe, French lavender and bay laurel
+ **Tender** (1°C–5°C/34–41°F): petunia, marigold, banana, oleander and citrus trees
+ **Heated glasshouse or grown outside during summer** (5°C–15°C +/41–59°F +): cymbidium, pineapple, bougainvillea, gloriosa and sweet peppers.

Above A cold frame made from brick and wood, against the warmth of a south-facing wall protects plants over autumn and winter.

Watch local weather reports or download an app on your phone to keep abreast of the changing climatic conditions in your area. This awareness will help you choose plants that complement each other throughout the seasons. Plan for year-round interest by selecting plants with varying flowering times and foliage colours, such as spring bulbs (daffodils) to fill gaps, pots and containers filled with herbaceous perennials and ornamental grasses, summer-blooming roses in borders and large containers and autumn foliage plants like Japanese maples. Grow a mix of deciduous and evergreen plants for visual appeal, even during winter when some plants may be dormant.

Protect your plants

Protect your plants from the worst winters by wrapping your pots and containers in old woollen jumpers, layers of recycled cardboard or bubble wrap, like a winter duvet; covering the soil surface with a thick 10cm (4in) mulch; or creating a wooden frame from recycled wood and stretching horticultural fleece over it to protect plants. Also, position all your pots together, up close to the wall of your house. The wall will act like a radiator, emitting warmth during cold nights.

Tender plants must be lifted and stored in a greenhouse, cold frame, potting shed or indoors. If left in the ground and small enough, they can be protected using a cloche made from a plastic drinks bottle cut in half, covering the crown of plants with an upturned bucket or even a clear

Top Concrete blocks and a plastic lid form a make-shift shelter. **Above left** An old wollen jumper tied around a pot protects the roots from frozen weather. **Above right** Bottles of all shapes and sizes have been used to make a greenhouse, even the downpipe.

umbrella from a bargain store as temporary cloches. Open the umbrella, push the handle into the soil, and cover the vulnerable plants. Remove the cloche, bucket or umbrella on warmer days and cover again before the temperature drops.

If excessive rain is due, protect your potted plants by placing them together and building a makeshift wall from cement blocks or reclaimed bricks on either side, then cover with a plastic lid from a storage box. Alternatively, for small potted plants, temporarily place them into a clear plastic storage container with the lid on.

To protect plants from the scorching sun and periods of drought, shade your plants using wooden posts and net curtaining. Make frames from wood, screw them together and wrap the curtaining over them just like a canvas for a painting. You can then place the frame on bricks or wooden posts, above your plants, to shade them.

Keep a journal

Keeping a gardening journal each year to record your observations is essential. Note down the following:

+ keep a visual record (photos on your phone or camera)
+ make a note of the plants and materials that were successful
+ highlight any plants that failed
+ record what the weather was like
+ note any significant changes in your garden, for example, if an area floods after heavy rain
+ observe where there are gaps in your borders
+ note the date you sow seeds and when they should flower; also when they actually flower and if they have pests and diseases
+ keep a note of pests and diseases in general.

Your historical gardening record becomes a valuable resource, helping you refine your gardening practices and make informed decisions based on past experiences. Adjust your planting strategy if you notice certain plants struggling in specific locations.

Remember, understanding your garden is a continuous learning process. Regular observation and adaptation based on your garden's unique characteristics will lead to a thriving, sustainable and self-sustaining outdoor space – and this really doesn't cost you anything apart from your time.

Gardening isn't just for summer

When it comes to the seasons, winter can be a cold, wet and freezing time, but a great winter task is planning for the year ahead. I often hear that many first-time gardeners (and some seasoned gardeners too – I have been guilty of this in the past) pop to the garden centre or nursery, fill up their trolley with stunning plants with which they have been seduced and then get home and plant them up without really getting to know what growing conditions those plants require or whether they can be planted together. My top winter tip is to plan your pots or borders before you go to the garden centre or nursery. Do your homework online or chat with other gardeners or gardening community groups, and then take a list of plants to the garden centre. Again, this stage is free of charge; it just requires your time to learn about plants and growing conditions.

I also advise you to keep things simple at the beginning of your thriftier gardening journey. Don't plant dozens of different varieties; stick to a handful of plants and get to know them. Once they are happy growing, in the right positions, you can add further plants. Build up your experience and knowledge slowly. Even if you planted only one new plant every month, by the end of the year, twelve new plants would be thriving in your garden.

Your garden as a safe and sensory place

Viewing your garden as a personal sanctuary allows for mindful contemplation and relaxation. Planning, observing and getting to know your garden will help you to create inviting seating areas surrounded by fragrant herbs or aromatic flowers. Elements like handmade wind chimes (made from old and recycled cutlery or lengths of downpipe hung and painted to mimic bamboo) or a water feature (made from a bucket dug into the ground and painted black inside as a reflective pool) will enhance the sensory experience and provide a tranquil escape from your hectic life. Introduce vegetables, fruits and herbs to enliven your gustatory and smell senses. Aromatic plants with intoxicating smells can bring back childhood memories and help relax or enliven you, while different textures from plants and materials will add a wonderful tactile element.

Pathways and surfaces should be clear, level and made from non-slip materials, like gravel or brick. Store gardening tools and fertilizers in a secure location, out of reach of children and pets. Choose non-toxic plants if children or pets frequent your garden. Create shaded areas with trees, arbours or umbrellas to protect against harmful UV rays.

Turn mistakes into positives

I'm first to put my hand up where mistakes have occurred, but I try to turn those mistakes into positives. When I moved into my first house with its small Victorian garden, I really wanted a manicured lawn, so I opted for bowling-green turf. Admittedly, this was more expensive, but I had an image in my head of a pristine green lawn. This was 35-plus years ago and we didn't know as much as we do now about resilient gardens and how to approach them. This lawn needed a lot of water and human intervention to get it looking perfect – it certainly wasn't a thrifty or eco-friendly or sustainable approach. I learned from this mistake: if I had the opportunity to do it all over again, I would ditch the lawn and fill the garden with native plants and cultivated cousins, mulch both borders and pathways with a permeable self-binding stone for a harmonious and cohesive feel, and I would make space to practise my yoga and meditation.

Your garden will be changing continuously over time as you learn, both by you gardening in it and by the addition of and propagation of plants and whatever the weather throws at it.

Above Mulching annuals and perennials with hardcore, turns a mistake into a positive.

Opposite Seating in an enclosed space surrounded by harmonious plants makes your garden feel safe and secure.

Laying the groundwork

There are a lot of expenses associated with being a gardener. The garden tools you'll need can be expensive, soil and bought compost do not come cheap, and nor do purchased plant supports. Thriftiness is about saving money, but it's also about organic, eco-friendly, sustainable practices that stop the use of shop-bought pesticides and herbicides. As our climate changes, water will become scarce during the warmer months and winters will be either drier or wetter for longer periods. Harnessing water and using it wisely will be incredibly important. Of course, you can't have a garden without plants, which can be expensive. Choosing the right plants, collecting seed and observing what grows in your neighbourhood will be key.

Pick the right tools

Getting the right tools is vital so that gardening is fun and doesn't become a chore. When selecting tools, shop around in garden centres and DIY stores. Handle them, walking around the store to get a feel for their weight and the materials used. If, after 20 minutes, your hands and arms feel tired, perhaps you need a lighter tool. If your wrist hurts from opening and closing a pair of secateurs, look for a version with a twisting grip. Perhaps you don't like the feel of cold metal, or you don't like the idea of treating wooden handles when you've finished each gardening job. Tools should be comfortable to use without putting any stress on your muscles.

Of course, you don't have to buy new tools. Boot sales, flea markets, auctions, local gardening clubs, local online communities and selling or advert websites can be excellent sources. If possible, always check them over before you buy. Ensure that the union between metal, plastic and wood is firm and secure, handles are still smooth or padded and that blades are clean and sharp.

Giving tools as a gift or passing them down through family makes them highly personal: the memories made from receiving and using these tools are priceless. Or you might like to buy and refurbish old tools yourself. Blades can be cleaned and sharpened with liquid detergent, sandpaper, diluted bleach, paper towels and an oil, such as WD40. For wooden handles, use linseed oil.

Create a spot for compost

Instead of purchasing a compost bin, make your own using reclaimed materials (see page 32). Place your compost bin on bare soil and in a partial- or full-shaded position, where possible. The soil is teeming with microorganisms, including beneficial bacteria and fungi, which play a crucial role in the decomposition of organic matter. Direct contact with the soil provides easy access for these microorganisms to the organic material and accelerates the decomposition process. Nutrients are also exchanged between the composting material and the soil beneath, which can be absorbed by surrounding plant roots, enriching soil fertility. The bare soil also acts as a moisture reservoir, regulating the compost bin's moisture content; in other words the soil underneath the bin helps prevent excessive drying out or waterlogging, creating an optimal environment for decomposition.

The soil provides a natural base with spaces for air circulation, resulting in better aeration and drainage, crucial for the activity of aerobic microorganisms that thrive in oxygen-rich environments. The soil acts as a natural insulator, preventing extreme temperature fluctuations and providing a stable environment for microbial activity. It can also deter pests and rodents.

Grounded compost bins made from natural materials integrate seamlessly with the surrounding ecosystem, essential for sustainability and biodiversity. Your composting process will become part of the natural nutrient recycling. This DIY approach to making your compost bin from a free natural resource reduces costs and promotes sustainability – a win-win!

Devote time to water

Rainwater is free. Collect it from gutters and downpipes and store in a water butt or any open container. Water butts with a tap at the bottom are great as this regulates the speed at which the water comes out, while open containers are perfect for dipping in watering cans. Introduce two watering cans, perhaps in different colours – one that will be used for dipping and watering and the other for applying weedkillers, if appropriate. Use this collected rainwater to water your plants and any houseplants you might have, particularly during dry spells. These simple additions reduce your reliance on mains water, lowering water bills.

You could also make a wonderful reflective pool that doubles up as a water dipping station, saving on space and money.

If you are using an outdoor tap with an attached hose, a great thrifty option for keeping your hose tidy is to fix a wheel rim, which can be found at a local breaker's yard, to the wall with a securely fixed bracket. Your hose can be wound around the wheel rim, keeping it neat and tidy.

Don't forget the seeds

Many plants produce seeds that you can harvest, save and use from year-to-year, for free. You may want to organize a seed swap with your gardening neighbours or the local horticultural society or gardening club. This will save you money on purchasing new seeds and introduce variety into your garden. You might even discover unique plant varieties that thrive in your local area. Always remember, however, that seeds turn into new plants, which, in turn, can produce numerous flowers, fruits or berries. So, only sow enough for you to enjoy, unless you plan on giving or selling some of your self-grown plants to help pay towards projects in your own garden. For the cost of some peat-free, multi-purpose compost and by reusing yoghurt pots or plastic fruit containers from the supermarket you can keep your costs down and still make money.

Opposite top Simple clay pots make the perfect reflective pools. **Bottom left** Vivipary occurs when seeds begin to develop before they detach from the parent plant. **Bottom right** Collecting seed in paper bags and envelopes for future use.

Craft your own plant supports

Fallen branches, bamboo stakes or repurposed wood and materials can be turned into plant supports, such as obelisks and trellis. Ensure the supports are sturdy and well-fixed before adding your plants. Obelisks can be formed by taking about five bamboo canes or thick, straight branches all around 2m (7ft) in length and inserting the bottom third into the ground, pot or container in a circular or square pattern. Collect the tops together and tie them with garden twine, old tights or stockings or braided strips of plastic cut from a compost bag.

When making a trellis from bamboo canes, branches or off-cuts of wood, again, choose pieces the same length and lay them out first on the ground in the pattern you want to create. A simple square grid pattern typically works best as you'll not need to cut them down any further. Tie them together at every point that they cross each other. The trellis can then be fixed to a wall using hooks. Hooking your trellis onto the wall is better than nailing or screwing as you'll be able to lower the trellis if you need to paint or clean the wall.

When supporting plants in borders, use bendable twigs, known as 'pea sticks', such as those from silver birch trees or dogwood. These are natural and will blend and become obscured by leaves and flowers as the plants grow. For bushier perennials, such as peonies, create a ring of twigs and branches.

Ingredients

+ Pea sticks, bamboo canes or straight branches
+ Twine

1.

Select off-cuts or prunings with single stems, thicker than a pencil, with smaller twigs at one end.

For bushy perennials such as peonies, push the single stem end of an off-cut into the ground deep enough so it's firm and stable, and repeat around the plant in a circular fashion.

2.

Try to weave some branches together to create a loose framework or cage support.

3.

For tall perennials, such as delphiniums or runner beans, or to grow cucumbers upwards rather than outwards, find tall, thick, straight(ish) branches or bamboo canes. Wedge one end into the soil. To make it a little easier to push into the soil, cut this end at an angle. Create a teepee and tie together at the top. As the plants grow, tie them in with twine or braided recycled plastic.

Think big and go for bulk

When you purchase items in bulk, the cost per unit or cubic metre is much lower than buying smaller quantities. This applies to a wide range of gardening products, from seeds and soil amendments to mulch, compost and fertilizer. Garden centres and suppliers often offer discounts on larger quantities as an incentive to move more product. Bulk items often come in large bags, tubs or containers that require less packaging per unit. This helps you save money and reduces the environmental impact of plastic or excess packaging material, aligning with more sustainable, thriftier gardening practices. Another cost-saving benefit of buying in bulk is the reduction in transportation costs. Constant trips to the garden centre to purchase smaller quantities of soil, seeds or other gardening essentials can add up, especially with rising fuel costs, so factor this into your costs.

When you buy in bulk, you're not just purchasing for the immediate season or project – you often ensure you have enough supplies for future gardening tasks. This is particularly important for perennials, long-term projects or if you're planning multiple gardening tasks throughout the year. Having an ample supply of compost, mulch or seeds readily available eliminates the need to purchase these items again in the short term, preventing any unexpected expenses or last-minute purchases.

Many bulk garden suppliers offer custom soil mixes, mulch blends or compost tailored to the specific needs of your plants. These blends are often more cost-effective than buying pre-bagged mixes designed for specific plants like roses, vegetables or succulents, which can be marked up for convenience.

If the bulk quantity is too much for you, perhaps chip in with neighbours, friends and family to lessen the expense.

Above Propagating plants, especially growing from seed, is a great way to grow your garden for very little, if no, money.

Plants for free!

I love growing free plants using natural propagation methods. Propagation aligns perfectly with the principles of sustainable gardening. By producing your own plants, you reduce your reliance on commercial growers and nurseries, which often involve significant environmental costs such as transport, mass production and chemical treatments. Instead, you can cultivate your garden at home with minimal environmental impact. When you propagate plants yourself, you have control over the health and quality of your plants from the very start. You can choose the healthiest, strongest specimens from which to take cuttings or divisions, ensuring that the new plants inherit these desirable traits. A little later (see pages 138–57), I'll guide you through some of the different forms of propagation and explain how to get the most from them. These methods are to take cuttings from your existing plants, allow seeds to self-sow, cut roots and leaves to grow new ones or dividing and transplanting herbaceous perennials. This saves money, as you can make lots of plants for free and create an endless supply of new plants using the ones you already have. Also, with their permission, you can take cuttings and collect seeds from neighbours', friends' or family's gardens. This is a lovely way to share plants, and if you end up with too many, you can return the favour by giving them one of your propagated plants or spare produce later on. It also gives the specific plants around your garden their own special story.

Get to know your fellow gardeners

Gardening involves a lot of trial and error, and it's easy to waste money on plants that aren't suited to your garden, the wrong type of fertilizer or ineffective pest control solutions. Local fellow gardeners can share their personal experiences, offer advice on what works best in your local climate and soil conditions and even point you toward cheaper, more efficient methods.

Join a local gardening club, horticultural society or community garden to share resources, knowledge, plants and seeds. One of the most immediate thrifty benefits of knowing fellow gardeners is the opportunity for plant and seed swapping. Sharing seeds or cuttings from established plants is often more reliable than purchasing commercially, as these are usually tried-and-tested varieties that have already thrived in your local conditions.

Sharing expensive tools and equipment is more accessible and affordable. When you have a network of gardeners, you can also leverage collective buying power. We once needed to hire a whacker plate to lay a new path, so we asked our neighbours if they had any similar plans and whether they would be interested in sharing the cost. We had to wait a little bit longer to undertake the work and hired the machinery for an extra day to fall in with our neighbours' schedules, but in the end, three sets of neighbours worked harmoniously together. Many suppliers and garden centres offer discounts for bulk purchases, which may be impractical for individual gardeners but very manageable for a group.

Planning for the future

Thriftier gardening is a mindset and practice that all gardeners should embrace. What we do today will affect or dictate how we garden in the future. With spiralling costs, food shortages, the loss of bird species, dwindling bee populations, infected or contaminated lands and soils, invasive weeds, rising temperatures and rainfall, creating a garden where we can unwind, feed ourselves and our families, attract wildlife and help beneficial pollinators can make a huge difference. If every gardener opts for a thriftier, more sustainable and eco-friendly approach, where the idea of recycling and minimizing waste is seen as positive, we can create green corridors that are vital for wildlife and, in turn, for pollinating our food crops, which will benefit us both physically and mentally.

Taking on a new garden or facing an existing, established garden can be overwhelming, expensive and a lot of hard work, especially in the first year or so. But as the years pass, your confidence will grow, gardening will get easier and before you know it, you'll look at your outdoor space with new eyes. An old sandpit built for the kids from brick or block when they were young, for example, can easily be turned into a raised bed in the future, by breaking up the bottom to allow for drainage and filled with soil or be turned into a water feature with the addition of a pond liner and a new row of bricks to bed on top of the liner edges. Yes, there would be the initial expense to build the sandpit, but for a fraction of the cost and very little wastage you have a thrifty new feature.

PLANNING YOUR GARDEN

You may be starting out with a clear picture of how you want your outdoor space to look, or you might not have a clue. It is exciting whether you have a vision or are still exploring ideas. Key design tips will help you maximize your space while being eco-friendly and minimizing waste. Budget constraints may mean you'll start your project organically, possibly working outwards from the back door or focusing on a vegetable plot. Having a plan is crucial, even if it's only a simple checklist. This allows you to be creative while staying organized.

Whether designing a garden for your own long-term enjoyment or even just to sell the property, planning, researching and observing will prevent costly mistakes. Although plans can evolve, taking your time is essential. Groundwork might take a year, but gardening becomes easier with experience. We are always learning when working alongside Mother Nature. Remember, plants may not always thrive, and setbacks like failed seeds or compost issues are part of the process.

Developing your garden in stages can help you manage time and budget constraints. Consider clearing, building and planting in phases, especially if doing the work yourself. Don't overlook sustainability – recycling garden waste or repurposing materials like old paving stones as hardcore or dug-out soil for raised beds can reduce costs and environmental impact. Local community groups are great for sharing or sourcing materials.

Creating your dream garden can be costly, but there are many things you can do to help reduce costs and create a rich sustainable and biodiverse space. Hiring a qualified garden designer (like myself) is not always the cheapest option and may feel like a luxury, but the expense may be justified as you will be guided through the intricacies of good garden design. However, as a thrifty gardener, I know you'll be itching to get out there, get your hands dirty and start planning. Whether you have a balcony, garden or large estate, when creating a garden there are some must-dos and definite do-nots.

Go with style

To determine what sort of garden you want, start by asking yourself all sorts of questions, such as:

1. What do you want from your garden?
2. Do you intend to offset food bills by growing your vegetables, fruits and herbs?
3. Do you want to be fully self-sufficient?
4. Do you want to be creative with style by recycling materials to create a sleek modern feel or a relaxed traditional style?
5. Do you want a garden full of flowers?
6. What will your outdoor space do for your lifestyle?
7. What style of garden do you want? A traditional cottage garden, a naturalistic garden, a modern or a Mediterranean garden?

The internet is the perfect place to research and find images that reflect these gardening styles. Study both plant selection and the hard materials used alongside them. To get plant ideas, visit public and open gardens as well as garden centres and specialist nurseries. A traditional cottage garden will mix ornamental and edible plants and use reclaimed or recycled materials, like bricks, broken paving slabs or bark for paths, while a naturalistic garden will focus on a biodiverse range of native plants, with minimal hard landscaping and turfed pathways.

Creating a mood board is a great way to start thinking about the spaces within your garden. For example, you might want somewhere to sit, so perhaps a patio or deck is required; entertaining friends and family might be at the top of your list, so think about comfy lounging areas with soft furnishings that you bring from inside, perhaps in a covered area using recycled wooden posts and trellis. Or it might be important to get from the house to the end of the garden or shed in a straight line without having to tread on wet grass.

This crucial research stage in developing your style should cover practical considerations, like pathways, placement of a washing line, the outside taps and, perhaps at a later date, where to put a glasshouse or cold frame.

Try not to mix up styles unless you create 'garden rooms', each with a different style and feel. You can blur the boundaries by weaving ornamental grasses throughout to give a sense of cohesion.

Above With so many garden and planting styles to choose from, from dry arid to tropical chic, go for one that suits your location, aspect, soil and climate, but also the aesthetic you want to achieve.

Practical considerations

Draw the shape of your garden and fill in where the house and its doors and windows are in relation to the outdoor space. Then, using coloured sticky notes, add in the garden elements you want to include: a patio, a path, some borders, a shed and any other garden elements that you want to include. Play around with shapes by cutting the notes to fit and moving them around the space. This will become your working plan. Start on paper rather than going outside and beginning to dig up areas or cut back existing plants. This will save you time and money without wasting resources because you have to re-do something later.

Elements of your garden

Think about everyday gardening considerations, such as where the mower and bikes will be stored, what will happen to the grass and garden clippings, where will you dry your clothes, and so on. As you do indoors, you can very quickly amass many items in a garden, so storage is key to keeping it looking its best all year round. However, many elements make up a garden and below are a few examples of things to consider. Expensive items like a greenhouse might not be possible at the start, due to budget restrictions, but if you think you'll want one in the future, plan an area for it now to reduce costs in the long term. Perhaps a concrete base for a greenhouse could be used as a seating area initially. See Time to Build, page 86.

+ Lawn (hardwearing, wildlife-friendly)
+ Path (choose reclaimed or recycled materials)
+ Patio or deck and seating
+ Borders and raised beds
+ Pots and other containers
+ Shed
+ Cold frame
+ Greenhouse (it can be a DIY project, using recycled items from skips, yard sales, house clearances, refuse tips or car boot sales)
+ Screening (either plants in the form of hedging or trees, or recycled materials such as wood off-cuts, gravel boards or wood sheeting)
+ Pond or water feature
+ Pergola, arch or arbour (made from fallen branches, prunings, logs, recycled trellis, recycled wooden posts).

Above A simple wood fence doesn't have to cost the earth. Install it yourself and you can save even more. Alternatively, opt for a living native hedge by planting young whips.

We all have boundaries

Next, look at the boundaries. Are they open or fenced off, low or high? Is there a wall? Are the boundaries in good condition, or do they, or a section of them, need repair? Do the current boundary elements visually and/or sound-wise block out neighbours? Creating new boundaries can be expensive, so the thrifty gardener needs to be creative when using reclaimed or recycled materials. A tree positioned in the right spot can block out an unwanted view, though they can be expensive (see 'Trees as an investment' on page 108). For a realistic idea of how your patio or seating area feels, sit down where it will be. Look around and see where neighbouring windows are. As you look up, imagine a tree blocking the view. It doesn't always have to be planted near a fence or wall. Bringing a tree closer to you will screen more of an area.

Perhaps you want boundaries within the garden to create 'garden rooms' using fences, hedging or walls. Dividing your garden into smaller areas actually makes your garden feel bigger, especially if you cannot see the rest of the garden while you're in one of the rooms. Using mixed, native hedging works really well for creating these divisions. You can buy young bare root or root-balled hedging in winter for a fraction of the cost of a potted plant. These plants are also easy to propagate, so you can even make new hedging for free.

Take stock of what you already have

In most cases, unless you have a new-build garden, there will be existing trees, hedges, shrubs and borders. If you can identify any of the plants already growing, make a note of them as they may indicate the soil type. Also, study any tree canopies, i.e. how much the tree reaches outwards from the central trunk, how much shade it creates on the ground below and whether the soil around the tree's base is workable or hard and bare. Observing the canopies is important, as they'll have a knock-on effect when adding plants and any soil conditioners.

Take accurate garden measurements and add them to your plan. With these measurements, anything you add or take out to create your vision should fit, and you won't incur additional costs for rectifying things later on. Ideally, never take a single measurement, but take running measurements, i.e. measuring and calculating the total length of a feature by cumulatively measuring its individual sections along a single line. Note whether doors and windows open inwards or outwards. If you're lucky to have bifold doors, measure them when open, as they will invariably encroach on your outside space.

Phase your work

You might need to phase the work you do in your garden because of budgetary constraints. But this is a good thing! Instead of spending all your money upfront on plants or materials that might not work, phasing allows you to refine your design as you learn what works best in your environment. It allows you to manage costs, time and resources effectively. Rather than facing a large financial outlay all at once, you can purchase materials, plants and tools as you go, and prioritize the most critical elements, such as soil preparation, planting perennials or building garden structures. You don't want to damage and, therefore, have the cost of making good any areas completed in a previous phase(s). You'll also probably want to enjoy your garden while working on it, so think about where reclaimed or recycled materials or propagated or new plants will go before you use them. Keeping your garden tidy will be key. Will the materials require protection from the elements? Also, how will you enjoy your garden between phases? It might be that the next phase will not start for some time, so you need to think about this before starting any major work. If there will be lots of waste to remove, remember that the fewer skips or other loads of waste there are, the cheaper and better for the environment it will be.

As you work on your garden in phases, you can observe how the space evolves, how plants grow and how weather or soil conditions affect your garden. This observation allows you to make informed adjustments to your plan as you go.

Above Pots, bags of compost, wooden stakes and more soon add up, so finding a designated area where you can store these wil help when it comes to phasing your work.

Budget

As a thrifty gardener, you'll be money-conscious and want to keep budgets low and in check, and as already mentioned, you might want to do things in stages because of cashflow. Admittedly, creating a budget is difficult, especially if you've never done anything like this before. Start by asking friends, family and neighbours if they've undertaken any gardening projects and how much they cost. And don't forget that there are essential things that you'll never see once your garden is completed, such as foundations or supporting structures. These take time and money, but you'll want to get them right from the start and ensure they are built to last.

New-build garden

Starting with a completely blank garden, perhaps a new-build garden with no plants in it apart from some weeds and turf, can be easier than facing an established garden. Such spaces could cost you more, however. Frequently below the turf on new-build sites you'll find a lot of rubbish and rubble, which must be removed before work starts. You might be able to bag it up and take it to the recycling centre yourself, but this will cost you fuel and time. Consider re-using these materials in your garden to keep costs down, for the subbase to patios and pathways, for example. If your soil is incredibly poor, improving it will take several years, so consider creating raised beds. This way, you can add fertile soil, but remember this will be costly, so see if you can share the costs of buying soil in bulk with neighbours, family or friends.

Screening is normally top of the list for new-build gardens. Pleached trees, i.e. trees trained with interwoven branches that create a flat, formal hedge-like structure on clear stems, look great, but they're expensive. You can buy young tree saplings and grow them on, which will take time, but perhaps a quicker and cheaper option is to make your own trellis and grow climbers from seed. Many annual climbers reach 3–4m (10–13ft) in height in a single year, so the annuals can soon cover any handmade trellis screening neighbours' properties, while perennial varieties get off the ground.

Many new-build gardens may not have external garden access, so remember that any materials, compost, recycled objects will need to go through your house.

Established garden

Established gardens are more complex. The best things to do for your budget when you inherit an established garden is to watch, take note and wait. Depending on the time of year you move in, you might not know what's growing in the garden. Use apps on your phone to help with plant identification. Your planting journal/diary is, therefore, essential (see page 49). Jot down what is growing in the garden and where at different times of the year. For example, herbaceous perennials will be underground during the winter. The same goes for bulbs. Take your time, as this will save you money in the long run. Unlike a new-build garden with no plants, you might want to save most of the plants, possibly replanting them in different areas. Tie string/ribbon around plants that you want to keep. If you are confident, you can propagate existing plants, having checked first that this is wise for a particular plant. Some plants, however, may be damaged or harbour pests and diseases; you'll need to remove them, otherwise, later on, you may have the additional expense of buying ingredients to make your own herbicides and pesticides.

Simple plant labels can be made from lolly sticks or by cutting up a plastic milk carton into strips and using an indelible ink pen to mark and label where certain plants are. But you might want to clear a small area and start growing your own vegetables, fruits and flowers. If this is the case, then approach this area like you would a new garden. Look at the soil and test it (see Feel the soil, pages 28–32) before sowing or planting. Being an established garden, you might need to enrich the soil, weed the area and gently fork over the soil, or follow a no-dig approach.

Above A new-build garden covered with cheap grass. **Below** An established garden rich in biodiversity and great for pollinators.

Above Portable folding furniture is ideal in rented accomodation, as well as growing everything in pots and containers, as you can take the lot with you when you move.

Rented garden

Taking on a rented garden or allotment will require the same observation and planning stages, but you won't want to waste money on items that you can't take with you if you move. You might not be able to change paving or fencing, but you can get creative with pots, containers and raised beds/mangers that can be relocated. Re-using old pots and containers – perhaps old metal food containers or stone or plastic pots that need some TLC (possibly spraying them all the same colour with weatherproof paint) – will keep the costs down and help your overall budget. Recycling household items means you can spend your budget on plants and furnishings. For very little money you can buy wheels or castors from DIY stores. Add these to the bottom of pots and containers and they become moveable items, which is great if you need to make more space on your patio, and easier when it comes to moving.

The key is to add elements that can be easily picked up and taken elsewhere, as and when required; something that becomes a little more difficult once pots, containers or raised beds are full with soil and growing plants. If you know that you'll be moving in 12 months or so, then don't opt for large fruit trees or large shrubs. Grow annual vegetables and flowers and try and work in a moving date with the harvesting or final stages of annual growth, i.e. when they are dead.

If you rent an allotment and get the allotment bug, you probably won't want to move far. You will need to take your time with this precious space. Don't use it just as an area to grow edibles, but create a garden and surround yourself with the plants that you love. Many rentals don't come with a garden, so being able to create a haven for you and wildlife on an allotment will be invaluable.

Finally, planting!

Buying new plants can be costly, but, depending on the time of year, there are alternatives you can consider. Creating a lawn in the spring or autumn can be expensive if you decide to opt for turf. It is perfect for an 'instant' garden, but if your area is large, then seed is the cheaper option. Also, being cost-wise isn't only about saving money. Think about the time of year with regards to your management of time. Spring and autumn are the best times for digging and preparing soil as it's soft, resulting in fewer hours of work. The soil might be more difficult to work with during the summer, especially if it's a hot, dry summer; spades can bounce off clay soils at this time, so you might end up having to hire specialist equipment and tools, which will be costly, so try and avoid this. Between November and March, many shrubs, trees, hedging and perennials can be bought as bare-root or root-balled plants (not grown in pots, but lifted direct from a field), which can be bought for a fraction of the price of a potted plant. Once planted, the plants' roots have time to establish quickly, or settle in, as more of their roots are in direct contact with the soil after planting. Potted plants can, however, go in any time of the year if the soil is not frozen or waterlogged, but rather than buying a 3-litre potted plant choose a 9cm potted plant. Admittedly it will take a little longer to grow, but within a few years, the 9cm potted plant will be the same size as the larger potted plant. Knowing the optimum times of the year will help save money and time in the long run.

Most gardeners are impatient. We want to enjoy our gardens and be surrounded by healthy plants. But an instant garden will require established plants, and the cost of these will eat into your budget dramatically. Watching plants grow, learning along the way, working out why plants have failed and keeping an eye out for pests and diseases are key to being a good gardener. As a thrifty gardener you'll be growing plants from seeds, cuttings or from young plants, so you'll have the time to observe your garden. You might want to follow trends and fashions in gardening and garden design, but invariably you'll grow what you like, what you enjoy eating and how the plants make you feel.

Below Plants can be expensive to buy, so start propagating your own from strong stalwarts in the garden.

When to call in the professionals

You might think that if you undertake all the work yourself, you will save money, but there are specific tasks that left to a professional contractor will save you time and money in the long run. Remember, thriftier gardening is not always about saving money by recycling materials, it's about saving money in general, being cost-wise and doing things right that will last for years to come. The table below highlights major tasks and advises whether you or a contractor can or should do them. Of course, with research and trial and error, you can achieve all of these tasks yourself, but it might cost you more time and money in the long run if you do them all yourself.

Task		
Clearing the site	**You**	Yes
	Contractor	Yes
	Results/ Cost Saving	You can undertake this work and cut costs of between £500 and £2,500 for a small-medium sized garden.
	Pros	Clearing it will help you get to know your garden; you'll have a real sense of achievement. You'll avoid contractors' disposal costs due to government regulations.
	Cons	It can be hard work, both physically and mentally.
Removal of large trees	**You**	No
	Contractor	Yes
	Results/ Cost Saving	Contractors have to be insured; they can do the work quickly.
	Pros	Contractors with specialist equipment will make quick work of this.
	Cons	To remove an average-sized tree costs £1,000–2,000. Safety is vital. Without the right tools you could harm yourself or worse. Removing the stump requires a stump grinder which only a trained operative can use.

Erecting new fences

You	Yes
Contractor	Yes
Results/ Cost Saving	Depending on the length of run or difficult topography, it might be quicker and cheaper for a contractor to undertake this work. Doing it yourself can save c. £2,000.
Pros	A great new skill to have.
Cons	Whoever does the work, height regulations must be followed. Thick/solid fencing could block natural light.

Building new walls

You	Yes
Contractor	Yes
Results/ Cost Saving	Depending on the length and height, it might be quicker and cheaper for a contractor to undertake this work. Anything over 1m/3ft or retaining large amounts of soil should be carried out by a contractor (and surveyor). Doing it yourself can save between £750 and £3,000 for a 1m high × 8m (3 × 26ft) long wall in brick, or between £250 and £600 for a 1m high × 4m (3 × 13ft) long wall in natural stone.
Pros	A great new skill to have
Cons	Walls must have firm, solid foundations and be laid level at all times (fences are more forgiving of slopes or changes in soil levels). It's a skill that needs to be mastered.

Foundation work for walls

You	Yes
Contractor	Yes
Results/ Cost Saving	Depending on the size, it might be quicker and cheaper for a contractor to undertake this work. You can tackle low brick/block walls yourself. It can save you between c. £160 and c. £300 per linear metre (around 3ft) for a trench foundation excavation.
Pros	A solid, level foundation will result in a wall that will last for years. You can use recycled materials, such as broken-up paving, bricks and blocks for footings keeping costs down and being more eco-friendly.
Cons	You'll need space for excavated soil and for placing materials. The average cost for ready-made concrete is around £150–£250 per cubic metre (35 cu ft).

Laying a patio

You	Yes
Contractor	Yes
Results/ Cost Saving	Depending on the size and type of material, it might be quicker and cheaper for a contractor to undertake this work. It can save you c. £150 per sq m (11 sq ft) if you do it yourself.
Pros	Recycled, square or rectangular paving is easier to lay than shaped paving. Selecting smaller paving or reclaimed bricks will make it easier to lay. Concrete paving is cheap and easy to lay (but not that eco-friendly). Slabs and blocks are laid on a level bed of sand and infilled with sand – easy and quick to install.
Cons	You need to observe where the water will run off the new patio and work out the standard ratio, 1:80, fall correctly. The larger the paving the more difficult it will be to lay.

Creating a path

You	Yes
Contractor	Yes
Results/ Cost Saving	You can lay simple paths of loose gravel or brick, but leave those using more expensive materials and any requiring compression from a water roller to a contractor.
Pros	Gravel is cheap, quick and easy to lay.
Cons	Resin-bound or bonded aggregate paths or self-binding gravel paths require specialist tools and know-how. For best results, you need to understand about slip resistance, durability of material and how each material should be laid.

Pergola, arbour, archway

You	Yes
Contractor	Yes
Results/ Cost Saving	You can undertake this work for most features like this. If the pergola is weight-bearing, consider a contractor/surveyor.
Pros	The sense of achievement is rewarding. You can use recycled or reclaimed materials.
Cons	For solid structures, post foundations will be key for longevity, and working at heights can be dangerous.

Water features, ponds, rills and waterfalls		
	You	Yes
	Contractor	Yes
	Results/ Cost Saving	You can build self-contained water features. Rills and water features that are not self-contained require a specialist contractor.
	Pros	Creating a pond yourself is very rewarding. Self-contained water features are quick and easy to install and don't necessarily need any foundations.
	Cons	Digging a pond is hard work. You'll need space for the excavated soil. Maintaining a pond can be time-consuming. Mixing electricity and water is dangerous.

Electrical work		
	You	No
	Contractor	Yes
	Results/ Cost Saving	Always use a qualified electrician.
	Pros	Qualified, registered and approved electricians have met all the required criteria to be awarded their status in accordance with approved industry practices and current statutory and non-statutory regulations.
	Cons	Safety concerns if you undertake the work yourself. Inclement weather and other environmental conditions must be considered and safeguarded against when undertaking any electrical work.

Working with different levels – steps and ramps		
	You	Yes
	Contractor	Yes
	Results/ Cost Saving	Using reclaimed and recycled products you can easily create steps, such as using recycled sleepers.
	Pros	You can get creative by using different materials. By doing it yourself, you can make step risers a size that suits you (min 10mm and max 18mm/½ –0.7sin).
	Cons	Digging the soil to make steps or foundations for a permanent, solid ramp is hard work. Building your own ramps is not always possible in the average-sized garden as 1 unit of fall requires 20 units of distance.

Sourcing containers and materials

Growing plants in pots and containers is practical and cost-effective. Skips, flea markets, car boot sales and recycling centres offer great options for finding affordable pots. Mismatched colours can be easily disguised, or you can turn them into a matching collection with creativity. Ensure pots are in good shape, and that you can add drainage holes if they lack them. Chipped pots can be positioned strategically or repaired. Bulbs, especially in lasagne planting (planting in layers), work well, along with annuals, biennials and perennials. Soft fruits like strawberries, raspberries and blueberries also thrive in containers, ideal for small spaces.

Give old pots and containers a second life

Sourcing pots and containers in a range of materials from coir, fibre, wool and plastic to metal, terracotta and more, is great fun. Give old containers a second life. Try using old metal cans of various sizes with holes drilled into the bottom for drainage – especially large commercial tins you might find on online marketplace sites or auction fairs. With the label either left on or removed or disguised, they make excellent contemporary-looking containers; there are also so many great-looking labels on cans and tins for things like biscuits, oils, coffee and hot chocolate. Every Christmas, there are many festive biscuit tins, and manufacturers often produce retro-looking tins when celebrating an anniversary – keep hold of them to add a splash of colour in the garden. Reimagine metal containers such as buckets, kettles and even saucepans to make decorative containers. You can even consider painting the tins with a metal paint to match existing pots and containers. I did this recently with some large white pots from our old Kent garden. As our new house is made of wood, the white didn't fit comfortably in the surroundings. I sprayed them all a warm terracotta colour for very little money. The paint also has flecks of metal in it, so the texture feels like a clay pot, too. New pots this size would have cost me hundreds to buy. Planted up and grouped, they give a fresh, cohesive feel and a riot of colour.

Other great finds to turn into functional and aesthetically pleasing containers include:

+ Sink – butler or Belfast
+ Chimney pot
+ Square chimney terracotta flue/liner
+ Metal bathtub
+ Metal or plastic watering can
+ Mop bucket
+ Coconut shell – especially good for hanging basket displays
+ Colander
+ Woven basket
+ Wheelbarrow
+ Car tyre
+ Kitchen mug
+ Bread bin
+ Metal water trough
+ Poultry-feeding trough
+ Cement block
+ Wooden barrel
+ Water butt or tank
+ Birdbath – great for alpine plants and succulents
+ Wooden crate or box
+ Hessian sack
+ Guttering
+ Enamel ware
+ Desk/sideboard drawer
+ Tiered fountain
+ Water cooler
+ Wire basket.

A trellis homemade from pallets, bicycle wheels, metal gates, bamboo canes or off-cuts of wood, with containers either attached to it or fixed to the wall, fence or railing, look extremely effective. Think about growing climbers and fruits, such as clematis, roses, raspberries, blackberries and even an espaliered fan-shaped peach tree. How good would it feel to step outside and pick your own-grown raspberries to add to your cereal at breakfast or a peach for a mid-afternoon snack? Raspberries and peaches are not cheap to buy, so growing your own, fixed to a homemade trellis, is a win-win situation. Even apples such as Cox's Orange Pippin or Discovery can be grown in recycled containers.

You can also grow acid-loving plants next to alkaline- or neutral-loving plants by selecting the right compost for each container.

It isn't rubbish!

If you have an old dustbin, don't throw it away. Circular or square bins can be easily disguised using reclaimed or recycled wood off-cuts, split bamboo screening on a roll or paint. You can even get slatted PVC bamboo on a roll, which can be a large sum to pay out on a tight budget, but it will require no maintenance. Cut the roll to the height of your bin and secure it in place with screws or tie them to the bin with wire or garden twine. Drill some holes in the bottom for drainage. These can then either be painted or varnished.

Above An old metal barrel makes the perfect pot for a young tree. The rust and weathered appearance adds character.

Large pots the size of a dustbin are perfect for shrubs and small trees. If you had to buy a pot this size, it would be costly. Another great thing about dustbins is that they are lightweight. Fill the bottom with recycled polystyrene from delivery packages and broken pots, gravel or stone to weigh it down (especially if growing a tall tree in it). Add some wheels or castors to the bottom (if it doesn't have them aready), and you have a pot that you can move around your garden or perhaps use it for screening.

Gravel boards and pallets

You can make bug hotels, bird boxes and more from wooden gravel boards (the piece of wood found at the bottom of a fence). You can create a simple but very effective wooden window box from a 3m (10ft) length of gravel board. Once built, remember to make some holes in the bottom for drainage and perhaps line the inside with the plastic bag that the compost comes in. This will extend the wooden planter's longevity, as it will not rot from the inside. Alternatively, use the boards to create planter boxes or shelves that can be fixed to a wall, fence or railing. You can leave these in their natural wooden finish or stain or paint them to fit your overall look.

Gravel boards and old pallets can also be used to build low garden tables. Why not build one with a square or rectangular hole cut in the middle, the size of a pot? Drop a pot (recycled of course!) into the hole and fill it with mouth-watering herbs or drought-tolerant plants, such as sedums and echeverias, or perhaps an alpine strawberry – perfect for picking when dining outside. Old pallets can be used for building several things, from raised beds to cold frames, but lent against a

Above left Old gravel boards can be screwed together on all four sides and the base. **Above right** Herbs can be grown in a wide range of recycled pots and containers, and moved around your outdoor space.

wall, the pallet's gaps between the slats are perfect for hanging pots from. Alternatively, add some wooden strips to the undersides of the gaps, line with a plastic bag and plant up with a mix of plants – you've now created a tiered planter.

Herbs for your plate and garden

Herbs require less space than larger plants, making them well-suited to grow in recycled pots and containers. Whether using small containers, old teacups or larger pots, herbs can thrive in these limited spaces, allowing you to maximize your gardening area, especially in urban settings or small gardens. They can also be grown in different-sized and shaped containers, ranging from old wooden seed trays to butter cartons, wooden boxes, plastic pots, hanging fabric shoe organizers and glass pots. Aim for a free-draining compost with added grit – ideally at a 50:50 ratio – as herbs hate having soggy bottoms! Additionally, many herbs have beautiful flowers, which tie nicely with other flowering herbaceous perennials in pots.

Herbs are relatively low-maintenance and adapt to different growing conditions, requiring minimal care, and if grown in lightweight pots, such as plastic or fibre pots, they are easier to move around for optimal sunlight or protection from harsh weather. Ensure they get a few hours of sunlight a day.

You can also cut plastic bottles (it doesn't matter the bottle's size, although the two-litre ones are best) in half, lengthways, to produce either mini cloches or planters. Fill with compost and plant up with herbs. Suspend the bottles on wires or fix to walls using brackets. Old guttering and wire can also create a similar effect.

Growing herbs in recycled pots allows for easy access to fresh flavours for cooking and garnishing. Having them on hand encourages experimentation in the kitchen, and the proximity of herbs can inspire more home-cooked meals, which is both economical and healthy.

Above Grow herbs in containers just outside the back door or a window for easy access.

Always keep the vertical in mind

Most outside spaces will have a bare wall onto which you can attach a bracket, hang a basket or another container, and grow a ball of flowers, fresh herbs or delicious trailing tomatoes or strawberries. Chain, cable and rope lengths can be bought fairly cheaply in hardware and DIY stores and attached to anything – just let your imagination go wild.

I remember seeing an incredible hanging glass container with herbs growing on a friend's balcony. When I asked where they bought such a stylish 'hanging basket', they laughed and told me it was an old fruit bowl. They asked at their local DIY store how to drill holes in the glass, and voila! But remember to keep it in a safe place just in case it drops (the chains on my friend's hanging fruit bowl thankfully looked very strong).

Above A simple raised metal edging, once bolted together, makes the perfect raised bed.

Materials and ideas for raised beds

Raised beds work very well in small spaces, i.e. gardens, on balconies and rooftops (but check the weight when full of soil and plants and when wet). Raised beds don't have to be all the same size or the same height. Consider having taller raised beds at the back and smaller ones in front; this way, you can bring colour up to eye level.

For a neglected corner of your garden or on a small balcony, recycle four different-sized old, chipped terracotta pots and a wooden stake/thick bamboo cane to make a small raised bed. Fill the largest pot with compost, then push the cane in the middle. Slip the next pot, slightly smaller than the first, over the cane and drop it down to sit on the compost. Continue with the next two. You can leave each pot as they are or angle them for a spilling effect. Plant it up, and you end up with a beautiful tiered mini garden, which can be re-planted for seasonal interest, or create your own herb garden or strawberry bed.

You can make raised beds from all sorts of salvaged materials such as: wooden pallets, scaffold boards, recycled wooden flooring, recycled fence panels, sleepers, old solid wooden doors cut in half lengthways, reclaimed bricks or blocks, stones or corrugated metal roofing. Old water containers also make excellent raised beds if you make some holes in the bottom for drainage. Disguising the plastic edges of these containers with reclaimed wood will give your raised bed a softer look. Ideally, line the edges of your bed with plastic, such as old compost bags stapled to the sides. For additional drainage, add rubble or broken-up pots, old slabs, polystyrene from delivery packages (only for growing ornamental plants, not edibles) or clippings from the garden. Fill to about half-way up the sides with garden soil or spent compost from containers. Then, fill the remaining half with a mix of compost, soil and organic matter. Apply an organic mulch to the soil surface to reduce weed growth, conserve moisture and regulate soil temperature. Use materials like straw, wood chips, homemade compost or shredded leaves, promoting a healthier soil environment without extensive disturbance.

Plants in raised beds are easily accessible for those with limited mobility. However, when considering spaces for wheelchair users or gardeners who prefer to sit when gardening, avoid flat-sided raised beds as they'll not be able to get their feet and legs under and garden comfortably. So, why not have a go at building your own raised bed on legs or 'raised table'. Recycle the trusty gravel boards, pallets or repurposed wood, and first build a box without a top. Next, reuse old table legs securely fixed to the bottom or add wheels to move around your outdoor space.

Other materials for raised beds:

+ Cement blocks
+ Sheet corrugated roofing
+ Bathtub
+ Washtub
+ Water tanks
+ Cleaned tyres
+ Bookcase (on its side)
+ Logs
+ Branches and twigs woven together
+ Storage bins
+ Large rocks
+ Straw bales.

Above/Below Raised beds made with wooden off-cuts and stone, both providing a different aesthetic.

Repurposing old furniture and household items

Thinking out of the box can be taken literally when it comes to repurposing old furniture and household items. Your home is already a treasure trove of goodies – all you need is some imagination! Place an old chest of drawers on a flat, firm surface, open the drawers to create a tiered effect, then put your plants, still in their pots, into the drawers, creating a beautiful mini garden (but weight it at the back so it doesn't tip forward). You can leave plants in their cheap nursery pots making them easy to take out and replace with something different. Or remove the drawers, fill them with soil and create separate raised beds/tables. Alternatively, the chest turned on its back and minus its drawers can be used as a raised bed. It will last a few seasons if the wood is in direct contact with the soil. I've even seen old dining chairs, brightly painted, used as plant pot holders – sometimes a leg is missing, but old bricks or books can quickly and effortlessly bring stability to an otherwise wobbly chair. If you have an accident with a mug that loses its handle, don't bin it; recycle it. Using a ceramic drill bit, carefully drill a hole or two in the bottom, fill it with compost, and plant a seed or fill it with a strawberry or an herb plant. An old office chair base works brilliantly when a wooden box is added, made from a gravel board – perfect for strawberries. Just such a planter was a key and much-loved element in my RHS Hampton Court Garden Festival Show Garden in 2023.

Above A repurposed colander has built in drainage holes, which makes it a perfect hanging basket.

An old plastic linen/washing basket can be used instead of pricey hanging baskets with pre-formed holes around the side to push plants into or for growing mushrooms. Once the plants have been fed and watered you won't see the basket for the flowers or mushrooms.

Used tyres can be stacked and painted to create colourful planters or garden beds. They are durable and can be used in various ways to add height and interest to your garden. Even old wooden or metal ladders can be repurposed as plant stands or trellises for climbing plants. Leaning a ladder against a wall can create an eye-catching display for pots.

When it comes to your tools, you'll need somewhere to store them. Metal or plastic buckets and bins can serve as planters or storage for gardening tools. They can be painted or left as is for a rustic look.

A pond

When we think of a garden, we invariably think of water. Recycle your old buckets or paddling pools (the firm plastic kind), which are typically left in the corner of the garden or behind the shed once the kids either get bored with it or have grown up. Or ask friends, family and neighbours if they have one. Make some holes in the bottom for drainage and sink the bucket or pool into the ground to create a pond to attract wildlife; add aquatic plants, pebbles for an accessible beach and large rocks. Alternatively, don't make the drainage holes; plant up a bog garden, with plants such as *Ligularia dentata, Persicaria bistorta, Pimula japonica* and *Matteuccia struthiopteris*.

Local suppliers

Sustainability and thriftier gardening mean sourcing materials ethically and locally for minimal environmental impact, reducing your garden's carbon footprint. We have become used to seeing a range of expensive exotic materials like tropical hardwoods, sandstone from India, marble and other paving materials from the Far East on social media and in magazines. But these are incredibly expensive and good sustainable solutions can be found by researching and finding local or nearby quarries for stone, chippings and gravel, reclamation yards and recycling centres for building materials. Make sure any timber always have the FSC (Forestry Stewardship Council) associated with it, which shows that forests meet the highest environmental and social standards. If you work with a local woodyard, the owner or landowner will probably grow their own local trees that are coppiced (cut to the ground) annually, providing a steady supply of posts and cut timber.

Get to know local woodyards and timber merchants and see if off-cuts can be bought cheaply or taken away. Some merchants have a corner where off-cuts are placed. These are sold at a fraction of the price and are sometimes referred to as 'grey timber'.

Seed sowing

Growing plants from seed is very rewarding, but you need something to sow them into. Any container with drainage holes will work. You can use recycled items like clean margarine tubs, yoghurt pots, takeaway trays, clear fruit punnets, egg boxes and toilet roll inners. You can also make purpose-built seed trays from a gravel board or off-cuts. Once your seedlings have grown, or you've taken cuttings or divisions from plants, you'll need to transplant them into individual plant pots. These soon mount up, especially if you're growing all your plants from seed and propagation methods. Old Yorkshire pudding or muffin trays work well, for shuttling all these potted plants as they are solid and lightweight. Of course, if you have a load of plastic nursery pots, don't bin them; reuse them repeatedly until they disintegrate. Also ask family, friends and neighbours if they have any plastic pots lying around, or if they can put some of their recycling items to one side. This is cost-wise and eco-friendly.

Above Getting started doesn't have to cost a lot. Tin cans, egg boxes and recycled plastic containers make the perfect seed sowing kit.

Planning the layout

When it comes to planning your garden, there may be features you already have and likely others you don't that you might want to include. Adding any single one of these features could drain your budget, but there are some clever design tricks and tips that you can use to make your budget go further, and help you to get the garden of your dreams.

Making sure you have an area or shelter in which to store items is an essential stage when starting to plan the layout, and one that many people forget to factor in. Without it, you'll find yourself moving items around your garden continuously, clogging up your layout. Planning is not just about what goes into your garden, but also about the mechanisms and approaches for making it easier to garden in and more affordable.

Listed in the next column are some of the features you need to think about when planning your garden. These include hard surfaces, barriers, screening, shelter, water features and ornamentation. Look at the list and apply it to your space:

+ paving
+ steps
+ decking
+ lawn
+ paths
+ hedging
+ walls
+ fences
+ gates
+ doors
+ barriers
+ water features
+ lighting
+ furnishings
+ shelter
+ shed
+ greenhouse
+ cold frame
+ screening
+ sculpture and ornamentation
+ sound.

I've mentioned previously the merits of sourcing materials locally from skips, flea markets, car boot sales, and so on. Of course, you're going to need somewhere to store this material while you start on your garden. Even if it might not be a priority, building a shelter or shed to store tools and materials is an excellent place to start. If you have a small outdoor space, then storage boxes can be bought for very little second-hand from car boot sales or new in sales at DIY and hardware stores. If you've sourced some old doors, windows and wood from a skip or from local advertisements, through social media, or local gardening clubs or

Above A garden shed allows you to store your tools. If you have space add a kitchen work surface, some OSB or chipboard to turn part of it into a potting bench.

community gardens, then building your own is both fun and practical. Think of a shed as a box. Securing the corners will need four corner posts or 'L' brackets. You could leave the front open, like a log store, as long as you have a roof of some kind with an overhang. The most accessible roof material is steel corrugated roofing sheets, and at around £11 per linear metre (around 3ft), it's a quick, efficient and budget-friendly way to keep items dry below. You might even be able to find second-hand roofing sheets online or through advertisements. If, later on, you have some spare money, or you save up and ask friends and family to contribute each year towards your birthday present of buying a shed or a cold frame, then the open store can easily be turned into a log store or even a sheltered place to sit. Doubling up on items and features is a fantastic way to be cost-wise. Planning this storage phase is therefore essential to the smooth creation of your garden.

Begin by outlining your landscaping goals. Identify areas that need immediate attention and prioritize projects based on urgency and cost. A clear plan helps you avoid impulsive purchases and costly mistakes.

Time to build

Every garden showcases design elements and materials that must be thoughtfully considered for a cohesive effect. Take photos and notes of elements you admire. If you like stone, brick or concrete, explore available types and their effects. For instance, different-sized aggregates in concrete give varied finishes, and can add grip to pathways or seating areas. While concrete is not very eco-friendly, it is cost-effective and easy to work with. Combine surfaces to create pattern and texture, but limit your choices to a few materials for a well-coordinated look.

Landscaping on a budget

Landscaping on a budget requires creativity and resourcefulness. Take on as many tasks as you can yourself, from planting to building garden features. There are plenty of online resources which can guide you through various DIY projects, significantly reducing labour costs. Choose native plants – often they are more resilient and require less maintenance, and will typically thrive in your local climate, reducing the need for water and fertilizers, saving you money over time. Use recycled or repurposed materials for hard landscaping. Old bricks, paving, stones and wooden off-cuts can all be transformed into pathways, path edges, raised beds or decorative features. Manage your costs while improving your knowledge and landscaping skills by starting with smaller projects, such as creating a flower bed or a container garden, before you tackle larger areas. Buy plants and materials in off-peak seasons when prices are lower. This, plus careful planning will help you achieve a beautiful garden on a budget.

Using concrete

Concrete can be extremely useful and beautiful, especially in a modern garden setting. A concrete garden bench can become a focal point and concrete makes a wonderful wipeable surface for an outdoor kitchen. It is a quick and useful material to use, but it's not environmentally friendly (although it can be recycled instead of going to landfill). There are new concrete alternatives on the market, such as hempcrete and bioconcrete, as well as biodegradable alternatives made from sustainable materials, such as mycelium (fungus) or agricultural waste, that offer similar structural properties. Do your own research; they may not be more cost-effective, but they are more sustainable and environmentally friendly.

To use cement to create a concrete base, first clear the area, removing any soil, stones or other debris so that the concrete pad will sit slightly higher than ground level. Dig out the base to a depth of 7.5–10cm (around 3–4in). This is shallower than what's needed for a driveway, garage or a commercially usable pad, as garden foot traffic will be lighter. Before laying cement, lay weed-suppressant membrane (old compost bags with drainage holes cut into them will work) and then a sub-base on top to separate the concrete and the soil. You can use crushed bricks and paving or MOT Type 1 hardcore. Builders or homeowners often want to get rid of hardcore (you may even have your own) so look out locally (or further afield but factor in transport costs). Create a frame to prevent the cement from spreading to other areas – known as 'shuttering'. Use off-cuts of wood and wooden pegs, or place temporary blocks around the slab's perimeter. Mix the concrete, ideally using a ratio of 1 part cement to 2 parts sand to 4 parts coarse aggregate (gravel/shingle). Then pour the cement evenly onto the hardcore sub-base and, while damp, smooth the surface with a length of wood. Finally, let it dry for 24 hours before removing the shuttering.

Minimalist gardens often rely on crisp edges and solid structures. With a brick or block mould, made from wooden off-cuts, you can also make your own cement bricks to build raised beds, fire pits, planters and low retaining walls. Many objects can be used as moulds to create concrete ornamentation. Old glass lighting globes (even plastic pots) picked up second-hand can be filled with cement. Once it has hardened, place the globe into a black bin bag and hit it with a hammer to break the glass. The resulting concrete balls can be used throughout the garden as sculptures, feet for low coffee tables made from recycled wood or as pot feet for large pots and containers.

Using imported stone or concrete will be costly and not particularly environmental; however, stone has a carbon impact of about one-third that of concrete, so always do your research. Always consider whether importing material with a high carbon footprint, due to the long distances it travels, is cheaper or more expensive for your budget and how it fits with your sustainable and environmental goals.

Quick and easy pathways

Loose materials, such as gravel, bark, recycled rubber or plastic chippings, or recycled tumbled glass, can quickly create great textural elements within your garden. Gravels tend to give a more relaxed feel and can be used efficiently for paths and driveways, creating gravel gardens or as a mulch in borders and containers to prevent weeds. To contain the loose surface material, you'll need an edging material. Brick, wood, stone or woven twigs and branches are all perfect for traditional and cottage-style gardens, while metal and wood edging work best for modern settings. You could even consider an edging of upturned glass bottles. Mulch or wood chip pathways are cheap and quick to lay. Lay down landscaping fabric or weed-suppressant fabric and cover with mulch or wood chip. Edges can be defined with large stones or logs. This type of pathway is ideal for areas under trees, children's play areas or around raised beds in a vegetable garden.

Stepping stones made from recycled paving, concrete blocks, linear concrete edgers or cinder blocks, laid in straight lines or a staggered pattern, requires digging an area the size of the recycled material and to a depth so that the paver is 1–2cm (½ – ¾in) proud. If necessary, level the soil with a layer of sand first.

The simplest pathway is one made from turf, especially if you have cut out areas for borders, and the grass has naturally become the pathway.

How to lay a gravel path

A gravel path is easy to create, especially on a budget. You will, of course, need to source some gravel, but keep an eye out for advertisements, group chats, community gardens or builders who are looking to get rid of any excess gravel. There are different types to choose from, such as crushed stone for excellent drainage, pea shingle which is soft underfoot, decomposed granite which forms a firm, stable surface, slate chippings that are perfect for creating a textured surface, limestone gravel that compacts well and provides excellent drainage or gravel mixes that often include smaller stones and sand to provide a stable surface.

Ingredients

+ String or a garden hose (to outline the path)
+ Garden spade
+ Rake
+ Bricks, setts or metal edging
+ Hardcore
+ Weed-suppressant membrane or recycled compost bags
+ Gravel

1.
Mark out the path by laying out string or a hosepipe to your desired shape.

2.
Use a garden spade (square-edged is ideal, but not essential) to remove any turf and topsoil and dig a trench to a depth of c. 7.5–10cm (around 3–4in).

3.
Rake over the bottom of the trench, then shuffle your feet over the soil until smooth.

4.
Install an edging, such as brick, setts or metal edging. Keep them in place using cement or surround with soil and gravel.

5.
Add a weed-suppressant membrane or recycle compost bags with drainage holes.

6.
Add around 10cm (4in) of hardcore (see page 87) as a firm sub-base. Walk over it to compact it and keep checking it is level.

7.
Shovel gravel onto the subbase, stopping around 3cm (1¼in) below the top of the edging.

How to lay a simple paved path

Laying a simple paved path on a budget can be a rewarding DIY project that enhances your garden's functionality and aesthetics. Not only does it provide a clear route through your garden, but it also adds a touch of style and character. Decide on the path's shape and width. A straight path is easier to install, while a curved design may require more planning. Choose budget-friendly paving materials such as concrete pavers, reclaimed bricks or natural stone. Consider visiting local suppliers, recycling centres or checking online marketplaces for deals or second-hand materials to save money while still achieving the look you want.

Ingredients

+ Tape measure
+ String or a garden hose (to outline the path)
+ Shovel
+ Spirit level
+ Tamper or compactor (make one by screwing a square piece of wood to the bottom of a broom handle)
+ Rubber mallet (for pavers)
+ Landscape fabric (optional)
+ Pavers or bricks
+ Sand or gravel (for levelling and filling gaps)
+ Edging material (optional)

1.

Use string or a garden hose to outline the path, ensuring it fits your garden layout. Remove grass, weeds and debris from the marked area, digging down around c. 10–15cm(4–6in) based on your paving choice. Lay the weed suppressant membrane or recycled compost bags with drainage holes.

2.

Fill the excavated area with 5–7cm (2–3in) gravel, sand or crushed stone. This layer aids in drainage and creates a solid foundation.

3.

Use a tamper or compactor to pack the gravel or sand tightly, ensuring it's level with a spirit level.

4.

If you're using pavers, spread a thin layer of sand 3cm (1¼in) over the crushed stone for levelling.

5.

Begin laying your pavers in the desired pattern, starting at one end and working your way across. Ensure they fit snugly, using a rubber mallet as needed. Regularly check that the pavers are level and make adjustments as necessary. Keeping to a simple pattern will reduce the number of cut pieces, which could save you money.

6.

Once all pavers are in place, fill the gaps with sand or gravel to lock them in and prevent movement. Sweep it into the joints and lightly compact.

7.

Install edging materials along the path's sides for added stability and a polished look if you wish.

8.

Clear away excess sand and debris from the surface of the path. Lightly mist the path with a watering can or fine spray on a hose to settle the sand in the joints, ensuring not to overdo it. Allow the path to settle for a few days before allowing heavy foot traffic.

Lawn alternatives

We love our lawns, but looking after one is time-consuming and, unless left long at certain times of the year, it does very little for wildlife, especially beneficial pollinators. If growing your own food and flowering plants to save on food bills and being more sustainable, lawn space could be used for raised beds and borders with simple bark-chipping or turf pathways. While many view a lawn space as good for entertaining, imagine holding a gathering among fruit, vegetables, herbs and flowers. Being surrounded by colour, texture and scent will undoubtedly make the space feel more relaxed.

Of course, if you are set on the idea of a lawn, use living grass, not artificial. Choosing the right turf is important. If you have kids who love playing outdoors, a family lawn turf will suffice and will be easy to maintain. For areas that are affected by adverse conditions, a more expensive turf will be better, as they normally bounce back well after prolonged dry periods. However, if you're looking for a really ornamental lawn, then a deluxe turf with fine-bladed grass is key, but this will cost you more. To achieve a healthy lawn, you must prepare the ground according to whether you are sowing seed or laying turf. Seed is a lot cheaper, and is a perfect choice if you can keep off the area while it establishes. Today, wild-flower lawns are popular, so why not sow some seeds and see what comes up?

Alternatives to the traditional lawn include a tapestry lawn: a diverse mix of grasses, herbs and flowering plants, creating a rich tapestry of textures, colours and ecological benefits. Grow perennial ryegrass, fine fescue, creeping thyme, sweet woodruff, sedum, ajuga, white and crimson clover, creeping phlox and Irish moss. Compared to traditional lawns, tapestry lawns often require less mowing, watering and fertilization.

Above *Soleirolia soleirolii* (mind your own business), and *Thymus* spp. (thyme) are great affordable lawn alternatives.

All these can be grown from seed very quickly. If you want to change your garden at a later date, the grass is easy to cut into, reshape, or combine with paving, such as stepping stones.

Adding height

Adding height to a garden can create visual interest, improve use of space and define areas without the need for extensive landscaping changes. Build simple wooden trellises or arbours to support climbing plants such as beans, peas or flowering vines like sweet peas and clematis. Create a vertical planter using wall-mounted pots or stacked planter boxes. This is an excellent way to grow herbs, flowers or small vegetables while saving ground space. Consider incorporating tall perennial flowers such as hollyhocks, delphiniums or sunflowers that will provide vertical interest, drawing your eye up to the open sky and making your space feel bigger. Also, varieties of ornamental grasses like *Miscanthus* or *Panicum* can add movement and height to your garden, creating an airy feel.

Above A simple wooden structure made from round poles and branches adds height and support to edibles and ornamentals.

Building raised beds (see pages 44, 80–81) not only provides height, but also improves soil drainage and provides easy access for gardening. Design your garden with layers in mind, placing taller plants at the back or centre of borders, depending on your view. This method creates a tiered effect, enhancing the overall height perception. Use garden stakes or poles to support various plants or flowers. You can tie climbing plants or vines to these supports to add verticality. Consider choosing stakes that are decorative in themselves or even repurposed items like old broom handles for added height and visual interest.

Lean an old wooden ladder against a wall and use it to display potted plants or trailing vines. A simple shelf unit can serve as a plant stand for pots, creating vertical interest on a wall or fence without much cost. You can hang planters from hooks or brackets attached to walls or fences. This is a great way to incorporate flowers and foliage without taking up ground space. And why not get creative with macramé plant hangers or wire baskets to suspend plants at varying heights.

DIY obelisks can be made from simple wooden dowels or bamboo poles tied together to create a simple yet effective height-adding structure. Build lattice panels or decorative screens as vertical features. They can serve as privacy screens while supporting climbing plants. Install a homemade trellis on a wall to grow climbing plants that will enhance the vertical height. Consider using stones, bricks or wood to create a stepped garden that increases height visually. This method is especially effective on sloped areas or hillsides. If you have natural slopes or mounds in your garden, emphasize them by planting taller plants at the top. Strategically placing large boulders or rocks can create natural height among planting, allowing plants to grow around them.

Share your garden with wildlife

Keeping our gardens thriving isn't just about adding plants that look good. We should also consider creating a home for native wildlife, as it contributes to the wellbeing of our gardens' ecosystem. Gardens can serve as mini refuges for wildlife, especially in urban areas with limited natural habitats. By planting native species, gardeners can provide food, shelter and breeding grounds for local fauna. Also, as mentioned in this book, native plants are significant because they co-evolve with local wildlife, making them better suited to support native insects, birds and other animals.

Create a haven

Wildlife requires food, water (such as in bird baths and ponds), shelter and somewhere to breed and thrive. In an urban environment, the collection of gardens, balconies and roof terraces creates a living patchwork, linking the outdoor spaces to the larger environment, the fields of growing food, the countryside and significant nature reserves. Many of our much-loved wildlife species are declining due to habitat loss, pesticide use and climate change. We can work with wildlife, though, by being thrifty, organic gardeners, considering our outdoor spaces as ecosystems and planting a range of plants for biodiversity. This connection or re-connection with nature provides an immeasurable sense of physical and mental wellbeing and grounds us in the here and now. This is known as the biophilic effect – or our innate need to be surrounded by nature and wildlife.

Healthy soil is the foundation of a thriving garden and ecosystem. Sustainable practices such as composting, mulching and avoiding chemical fertilizers enhance soil fertility and structure. These practices also support beneficial soil organisms like earthworms, bacteria and fungi, which play crucial roles in nutrient cycling and plant health.

Pest control

Sharing your garden with wildlife is not only beneficial for the environment but also a strategic approach to natural pest control.

Many wildlife species, particularly birds and beneficial insects like ladybirds and lacewings, are natural predators of common garden pests, such as caterpillars and aphids. Predatory insects, such as spiders and predatory wasps, target pests like aphids and whiteflies, effectively reducing their numbers without the need for expensive chemical pesticides. Encouraging wildlife introduces natural competition for resources among different species. When a variety of insects inhabits your garden, they compete for food sources, which can help control populations of pest insects that may otherwise proliferate. Working with nature, therefore, is common sense for the thrifty gardener.

Make room for bees and bugs

You can make your own bug hotel from a gravel board and materials found in the garden, such as leaves, twigs, bamboo canes, pine cones, broken pots and roof tiles. Bits of wood are great for ants, pine cones are great for ladybirds and green lacewings, a single slit is suitable for butterflies, round stems are good for beetles, and leaves, wood chippings and barks are good for earwigs.

Beetles and centipedes love wood piles. Fungi will grow on the wood that will attract more beetles and other invertebrates, which, in return, will eat slugs and slug eggs, and use the pile to raise their

Above Slugs and snails – a gardener's worst enemy or favourite ally? Every living creature has a part to play in your garden.

Top left An elegant painted bug hotel with a living sedum roof. **Top right** A bug hotel with bamboo canes and holes, as well as straw and dried leaves – perfect for solitary bees and beetles. **Above** A simple pile of logs and branches makes the perfect home for toads.

young and shelter from bad weather. Log piles are also great for amphibians and lizards, as the dead wood attracts insects, which they feed on. Allow vegetation to grow around and through the log pile to provide more shelter and increase the variety of insects.

Honeybees live in hives, but solitary bees make nests on their own and lay their eggs in tunnels, such as dead wood, soil or bamboo canes. You can make a bee hotel by tying bamboo canes together and hanging them from a branch. These bees will also use mud to create a cell wall along the tube. Plant diversity and continuous blooming will provide nectar and pollen through the year for such bees and other pollinators.

Make a gravel board box as your own butterfly home. Cut slots as entry points in the front and sand down with sandpaper. Fill the home with branches and leaf litter from your garden. Butterflies like it dark inside and prefer protected and sheltered areas in the garden. To attract many butterflies, surround it with flowering plants and ideally position it 60–90cm (24–36in) above the ground.

Pile up leaves

A simple pile of leaves is fantastic for wildlife. The leaves provide shelter and an excellent nesting spot for hibernating animals like hedgehogs, frogs and insects. Birds will also peck through leaf piles for a tasty meal of insects and worms.

Your feathered friends

Creating the habitats that wildlife need is essential. Leave seedheads over autumn and winter for birds to feed on. Put up bird boxes and feed them to attract a wide range of our feathered friends. You can make your own bird food using kitchen staples, such as suet or lard, sunflower seeds, chopped unsalted peanuts, oats, grated cheese and raisins. Mix into a ball and hang from a tree or smear it on branches.

Above An affordable handmade wooden birdbox positioned around your garden attracts a range of birds to your garden, such as robins.

Simple ideas and design solutions

Keeping your layout simple creates a practical, functional and aesthetically pleasing garden. Budgetary restraints can be seen as a positive, as you'll need to work on existing areas before starting on something new. Try to come up with creative solutions – simple, creative resolutions can often produce effective design solutions. Think about the points below, which don't cost you anything, but will give your garden that designer look without the price tag.

Shape and proportion

Wherever you look there are shapes and lines, from the architecture of surrounding buildings to the shape of the plants growing around them. How you put them together to create balance and proportion is as important outside as it is inside. When it feels right, you create balance. The Chinese principle of yin and yang is precisely this, as is feng shui – the practice of arranging items in living spaces to create balance with the natural world. When it comes to gardens, the same principles apply.

Use your house as a guide

You'll create a harmonious and cohesive garden by relating the shapes and proportions to the house. Are there strong lines leading off the house (sight lines) from the windows and the doorways? If so, extend these into the garden. Next, look at the shape of the your house and mimic the shape and proportion in your garden. If you have a bay window, say, use its shape and measurements to lay out and create new borders.

Use perspective

In the wider world, you'll see that objects look smaller the further away they are, and lines may converge at a single point. You can use perspective to give your space depth, accentuating lines and shapes to make a space feel longer or broader. A small sculpture at the end of a pathway will make the space feel longer, but one twice the size will shorten the distance as you look at it. You can make a garden look longer by narrowing a pathway in the distance to play tricks on the eyes. You'll only notice this narrowing when in that area.

Enable movement through your garden

Reclaimed and pressed concrete pavers, poured concrete, stone flags, decking, loose surfaces such as gravel, wood and bark chippings, grass, brick, cobbles, clay pavers, interlocking pavers, granite setts or Belgian blocks can all be used to enable movement. The function of the paving will decide the material and shape to choose, while the texture will dictate its practical use. For example, to get from house to shed, a straight path using a level paving material works best.

Create a seamless feel

Look at the internal décor where your outdoor space leads off from and choose colours, materials, pots, plants, furnishings and textures that complement it. This will create a seamless feel and make both indoor and outdoor space feel larger. Planting pale-coloured flowers further away from your windows and doors and brighter and bold flowers closer to the house will also give the illusion of depth.

Plan for interest for 12 months of the year

As a rule, you want taller plants at the back and smaller plants at the front, but now and then, it's good to dot taller, airy plants towards the front to look through to see the rest of the border. Aim for a good mix of mounds and spires and play off different textures, shapes and forms to the best effect. Colour choice is very personal, so try combinations and learn from your mistakes. I always work in layers when designing a border.

1. Underground, there are bulbs, corms and rhizomes. With the right choice, you can have shots of colour throughout the year.
2. Ground cover, small, low-growing plants knit together, supress weeds and retain moisture.
3. Herbaceous perennials, annuals and biennials give a floral flourish.
4. Climbers add height.
5. Shrubs and trees give impact, permanency, interest, shape, form, colour and scent.

Maintenance is essential

Keep on top of weeds and deadhead plants to prolong flowering (but leave some seedheads for winter interest). Some of your plants will need staking. Trying to add supports when plants are fully grown is tricky, so position any stakes when you plant so you can tie into the stake as the plant grows. Feed your plants throughout the seasons and label them or make a plan in your gardening journal, as you will forget what grows where.

Think about lighting

Lighting can transform a garden by underlighting trees or ornamentation, illuminating the way and making the garden a safe place to move about at night. Use lighting to create dramatic silhouettes, shadows and contrasts; highlight a feature to reveal its texture, material or colour; draw your eye to something; highlight branches and stems of plants; and to create a magical feel in water features as the water sparkles and moves.

Temporary lighting in the form of hanging lights can be solar-powered, connected to an electricity source or battery-operated. Fairy lights can be wrapped around trees, scattered over hedging and shrubs, and hung from pergolas, arbours and parasols to create a magical effect. Outdoor table and floor lamps can be plugged into a waterproof socket, enhancing indoor–outdoor living. Flames from candles, firepits, log burners or torches can provide cosy, atmospheric lighting.

Finishing touches

As they do indoors, the finishing touches make all the difference. Use recycled materials to create something personal to you that complements your style, be it soft furnishings or sculpture.

CHOOSING YOUR PLANTS

Plants make a garden, but with an estimated 390 plant species in the world, of which 250,000 to 300,000 are flowering plants, plant selection can be daunting. Where do you start? Consider the size of your garden and the space you want to fill. Larger plants can make a big impact, while smaller plants can be used as fillers or in borders. Identify your essential plants and allocate your budget accordingly, focusing on key feature plants, and then look for fillers. A good mix can be used to create layers and a balanced planting scheme.

To understand plants, you'll need to do some research and planning. Study the growth habits, maintenance needs and pest resistance of potential plants. Knowing which plants are likely to thrive in your environment will prevent costly mistakes. Sketch out your garden design to visualize how different plants will work together. This will help you avoid overcrowding and ensure a cohesive look.

Decide how much you're willing to spend on plants. This will guide your selections and help you avoid impulse purchases that could derail your budget. Plants that are essential might include those that serve a specific function, such as vegetables or native plants to attract pollinators. Allocate a portion of your budget for feature plants to serve as focal points. If a particular plant is too expensive or unavailable, consider alternatives that offer similar colours or textures at a lower cost. Don't be afraid to adjust your plant selections based on what is available and affordable. Sometimes, embracing local or seasonal plants can lead to delightful surprises. Keep a running tally of your expenses to help you stay on track and adjust as needed to avoid overspending.

Buying established potted plants can be expensive, so propagate them wherever possible. Bare root or root-balled plants also save money. Wise plant choices are those that are multi-purpose: offer year-round interest; look, smell or taste good; attract wildlife; or mine the subsoil for elements and minerals and make them available to nearby plants.

Thrifty plants

Being thrifty about plants doesn't necessarily mean buying cheap plants or rescuing them from the garden centre or nursery, although these help. Budget-friendly options often include native species, perennials and plants that are easy to propagate. They require less water and maintenance, reducing ongoing costs. Thrifty plants also promote biodiversity and support local wildlife, creating a vibrant ecosystem in your garden. By focusing on cost-effective, low-maintenance choices, you can allocate your budget to enhancing your garden in other ways, such as soil improvement or creating garden features. Overall, thrifty plants offer a sustainable way to create a beautiful and resilient garden without overspending.

Do your research

Find out what your chosen plant's final shape, height, spread, form, colour and texture will be, as this will dictate how far apart you'll need to position your plants and what you can pair them up with. By selecting a mix of deciduous (including those with interesting stem colour or autumn leaves) and evergreen plants for solidity with seasonal interest, you can work in the rest of the plants as infills. Mixing plants and coming up with plant combinations is great fun. As you learn more and get to grips with the basics of gardening, you'll find that selecting plants will become second nature to you.

Multi-purpose plants

Choosing plants with multiple uses means you'll need fewer plants initially and this will save you money. Repeating the planting throughout your garden is both cost-wise and aesthetically pleasing. Plants with multi-seasonal interest, such as spring or summer blossom, autumnal shades and textural bark that can be admired over the winter, are essential for your thrifty garden. Mixing plants that look good and are edible, whether it's petals (marigold, pansy or lavender), berries (blueberry, bell pepper or cranberry), leaves (chard, oregano or rosemary), seeds or fruit (poppy, strawberry or kiwi) or stems (chives rhubarb or sunflower), make it easy to follow the

Above Surrounding yourself with plants and creating little seating havens are only achievable once you know what type of soil you have. Look at the larger landscape to get inspiration.

cottage gardening principle of leaving no bare soil. Also, if, like me, you love growing flowers and stems for the garden and home that can be cut regularly without leaving gaps in your pots and borders, choose plants like cosmos, rose or dahlia that give you bucket-loads of flowers to enjoy indoors; these plants are multi-purpose, functional and beautiful.

Think soil

If you have poor, stony soil, plant herbs such as rosemary, sage, thyme and oregano, as they like free-draining soil. In chalky soil, plant drought-tolerant perennials that prefer alkaline soils. However, if you have heavy clay soils, loosen it up with organic matter and horticultural grit and choose plants that grow well in heavy clay and tolerate wet conditions. You can also consider adding a raised bed filled with a different soil type. If your soil is loamy, lucky you, as this well-drained soil type is perfect choice for many plants. The following plants work well in different types of soils:

Chalk soils ceanothus, clematis, dianthus, geranium and lavender

Alkaline soils rhododendron, pieris, calluna, enkianthus and erica

Clay soils mahonia, hydrangea, viburnum, sorbus and astilbe

Wet soils iris, *Crataegus*, *Lobelia cardinalis*, *Weigela florida* and actaea

Sourcing plants

Asking family, friends and neighbours if you can collect seeds or take cuttings from their plants is a great way to keep costs down, but never take cuttings without the owner's consent. Ensure you have a clear plastic bag and a sharp, clean knife scissors or secateurs to take the cuttings. When collecting seeds, take a paper bag or envelope. With cuttings, you'll need to prepare them and get them planted as soon as possible before they wilt. Also, many plants can be divided in the autumn, so if you've always admired a hardy geranium in your friend's garden or loved a bearded iris in your parents' outdoor space, then ask them if you can divide the plant for them and take a piece home with you.

Propagate

Using plants that are easy to propagate is a cost-effective way to expand your garden. Buying one of each plant means you can grow it on and propagate from it using methods such as seeds, cuttings, grafting, budding, divisions and layering (see pages 138-57), producing plants to add back to your garden. Propagating plants fosters a deeper connection to your garden and encourages sustainable practices by minimizing waste. By cultivating a variety of propagated plants, you can create a diverse and thriving garden while significantly reducing your overall gardening costs. Popular choices include herbs like mint and basil, as well as perennials like daylilies and sedums. These plants often root quickly, making them ideal for beginners and the cost-wise. Buy plants when they are small, in 9cm (3½in) pots, from local nurseries and garden centres in spring or early summer, as they will be cheaper than buying a more mature plant in a larger pot. By the end of the first year, hardy perennial plants such as catmint, hardy geranium and euphorbia will probably reach 60–70 per cent of their mature size. Another tip is to look closely at potted plants for sale, as you might be able to divide them before you plant them.

Above Coir or fibre pots are perfect for growing plants, such as cosmos, from seed.

Build a backbone

Shrubs and trees are the backbone of any garden, especially the thrifty garden. They create the framework, establishing its overall design and layout. They provide vertical elements that break up flat spaces, offering height and scale to the landscape. Flowering shrubs and trees and those with colour-changing leaves, berries, scent and texture, will help fill a border, pot or container and provide interest throughout the seasons, making them great value for your garden. They are also low-maintenance and generally pest and disease-free and you can easily make more plants for free by propagating them. Maple, rose, hawthorn, berberis and hydrangea are good examples.

Go perennial

Herbaceous perennial plants are great value for money as they come back year after year and are easy to propagate from; however, while your cuttings or smaller plants are growing, especially in the first year when you'll be doing a lot of groundwork, you can, for less than the cost of five standard coffees from a well-known coffee-house, for several packets of annual seeds fill borders, pots and containers with annuals such as cosmos, poppy and cornflower. Although these will flower in the first year and at the end of that year self-sow, and therefore every year after that, you can collect the seeds and sow them again in autumn or spring. They make wonderful partners to perennial plants.

Perennial bulbs are a great way to add colour and interest and are relatively cheap for the number you can grow. Choose spring-, summer-, autumn- and winter-flowering bulbs. When you receive your bulbs or select them at a garden centre, give them a squeeze and look for any signs of rot. They should be plump and firm to the touch.

Use grasses

Ornamental grasses are excellent for repeating throughout a garden and blending contrasting colours. Using grasses in the garden adds texture, movement and visual interest throughout the seasons. They provide a soft, natural look and can serve as focal points or elegant backdrops for flowering plants. Grasses are low-maintenance, drought-resistant and often require less water than traditional garden plants, making them eco-friendly choices. Their diverse heights, colours and forms allow for creative combinations in your garden. Additionally, ornamental grasses can attract wildlife, offering habitat and food for birds and insects. They can quickly grow from seed or by lifting and dividing the clump in early spring.

On the veg patch

Vegetables and fruit are easy to grow from seed. Ideally, the soil should always have something growing, so bare patches can be sown with quick-crops, such as radish, lettuce and beetroot, to fill the gaps. Remember to rotate your crops to keep soil-borne pests and diseases at bay (see Grow your own, page 23). Growing companion plants, like marigolds, lavender, nasturtium and sunflowers, will attract pollinators to your garden and encourage a balance of predator and prey species. This will result in fewer situations requiring the use of herbicides and pesticides, many of which are not eco-friendly or sustainable. Various plant species also disrupt the lifecycle of pests and diseases, reducing the risk of widespread infestations.

Above Ornamental grasses blend colours and textures seamlessly.

Don't be too tidy

Leave areas of the garden a little messy. In recent years, so-called weeds have appeared as cultivated plants in Show Gardens at the RHS Chelsea Flower Show. Remember, a weed is just a plant in the wrong place. Many are good for wildlife so why not have a 'weedy corner', hidden from view by a trellis or screen? Many weeds are edible, too – saving you money, but please check before eating. These are some of the 'weeds' you might want to keep.

1. Dandelions are brilliant for bees. The bright yellow flowers start appearing in early spring, and continue right through to autumn, so are a readily available year-round source of nectar. Butterflies and hoverflies like them too, and goldfinches feed on the seeds. Dandelions are edible for humans too: leaves can be eaten in salads; they are high in antioxidants and act as a diuretic, rich in vitamins, calcium, potassium and iron.

2. Daisies, buttercups and clover also attract bees, butterflies and hoverflies, so leaving a small area of your lawn uncut is a good way to help wildlife and attract vital pollinators.

3. Long grass is an excellent habitat for nesting bumblebees.

4. A nettle patch can support over 40 species of insects, and the plants provide food for caterpillars, so they are particularly good for butterflies, especially small tortoiseshells and peacocks. Nettles are edible for us, too. They have the same nutritional value as spinach and are high in iron, magnesium and calcium (don't worry, the sting is lost when cooked).

Above Leaving areas of your lawn long is great for wildlife. A simple mowed path, costs nothing but your time. **Opposite** Not cutting back seedheads in the autumn allows small insects such as this ladybird to nest down for winter.

Planting styles

Planning your planting is a personal thing. Other gardeners might use the same plants as you, but how you put them together will differ, depending on taste, style and function. The thrifty gardener is always thinking about sustainability, being eco-friendly, saving money, using money wisely and creating a rich, biodiverse space where edibles, edimentals and ornamentals live side-by-side. Cottage gardens or naturalistic gardens, therefore, lend themselves to the thrifty gardener. Our ancestors, before and during the Industrial Revolution, understood the importance of combining and growing plants close to each other – a beautiful rose would sit next to marigolds and cabbages and every piece of soil would have something growing in it leaving no bare patches of soil. Remember that the intricate web of relationships between plants, animals and microorganisms forms a resilient fabric that can absorb and recover from disturbances, including those exacerbated by climate change.

There are many different ways in which to use plants. Think about the following recommendations to help you plan your planting to suit you and your garden:

+ Group plants as a single connected block for a bold effect.
+ Place plants randomly within a border to create a more naturalistic effect.
+ For prairie-style planting, use the 70:30 ratio: 70 per cent grasses and 30 per cent herbaceous perennials – all of which can be grown from seed.
+ Plants can be used as punctuation points, accentuating shapes and patterns.
+ Plants repeated lead the eye through a planting scheme and garden.
+ Aim for a mix of mounds and spires, such as *Alchemilla mollis* and *Stachys byzantina* next to *Verbascum* spp. or *Delphinium* spp.

Above Make your outdoor space work for you. If the same palette of plants was given to different gardeners, every creation, planting style and combination would be different.

+ Think about the scale of the plants compared to the house and remember that plant foliage adds colour, texture and movement. Small, low-growing plants next to a large house look wrong, swamped and ineffectual, while larger shrubs and taller plants will have presence and sit comfortably next to a large house.

+ Some plants are architectural and make statement pieces, such as the spiky leaves of cordyline or aloe.

+ Select plants that have already adapted to the environment, require less watering and fewer pesticides.

+ Garden organically to attract a wide range of wildlife, keeping your plants healthy and pest- and disease-free.

+ Aim for a wide range of plants. Diverse plant communities are more productive and resistant to environmental stressors.

+ A diverse mix of plants acts as a natural buffer against the unpredictability of climate change. Incorporating native plants and those adapted to the local climate enhances a garden's resilience.

+ Be mindful of plant choices to avoid introducing species that may become invasive and outcompete native flora.

Trees and shrubs

With careful selection, trees and shrubs can provide lasting beauty and resilience to your garden. Every garden needs a mix, but mature plants are expensive to buy. Many can be grown from scratch, and for the thrifty gardener, shrubs and trees with more than one season of interest make sense. You can choose both evergreen and deciduous kinds; many provide shelter and food for wildlife, providing biodiversity in your garden, while others create natural privacy screens, offering shelter from wind, noise and prying eyes.

Trees as an investment

Planting trees is a long-term investment but watching them grow brings great satisfaction. Cost-wise, I see trees as a beneficial investment as they bring immense value to gardens in the form of environmental, ecological, aesthetic and emotional benefits. Specifically, they can add height, shade and shelter to gardens. They act as natural carbon sinks, improving air quality, cooling the garden through shade and transpiration and aiding in water management by absorbing rain and preventing erosion. Ecologically, trees support biodiversity, offering habitats and food for birds, pollinators and mammals, while their leaf litter enriches soil health, benefiting the entire garden ecosystem.

Aesthetically, trees create structure and scale, framing views, dividing spaces and adding year-round visual interest through seasonal changes in foliage, flowers and bark. Their forms, textures and colours elevate a garden's sensory appeal, with species like birch or maple adding unique visual and tactile dimensions. Trees also offer significant mental health benefits, as spending time around greenery has been shown to reduce stress and enhance wellbeing.

Culturally, trees often carry heritage and memory, living symbols of resilience and continuity. They can boost property value and lower energy costs through natural shading. By choosing trees that suit your garden's size and conditions, you can create a resilient, beautiful and ecologically rich space. Whether providing privacy, beauty or a connection to nature, trees are foundational to any garden, offering benefits that grow with time.

Choosing trees and shrubs

Trees and shrubs vary greatly in size, from dwarf varieties to towering giants, and come with many appealing attributes including striking flowers, fruit, foliage and bark textures. Trees can be purchased fully grown or as young plants, bare-rooted or as trained specimens like espalier or pleached trees for smaller spaces. When selecting trees and shrubs, it's important to assess the suitability for your space to avoid overcrowding.

Trees should be chosen with their long-term growth in mind, considering their mature size, root spread and sunlight needs. Shrubs offer more flexibility and can be moved or pruned to refine the layout of a garden. Together, trees and shrubs complement each other: trees provide the overarching structure and presence, framing views and offering privacy, while shrubs add seasonal charm and adaptability, ideal for borders, hedges and ground covers. Shrubs also adapt well to pruning, and can be shaped for smaller gardens or seasonal changes.

Trees and shrubs can be propagated through seeds, grafting, layering or cuttings. They come in a variety of forms: evergreen, deciduous and semi-deciduous, and some are drought-tolerant or salt-tolerant. Depending on the species, trees and shrubs can bloom in spring, summer, autumn or winter, providing year-round interest. When selecting trees, consider their shape: conical varieties, like tassel cherry (*Prunus litigosa*), are great for small gardens, while wide-spreading canopy trees, such as Indian bean (*Catalpa bignonioides*), are suitable for larger spaces. Other tree shapes include bushy, contorted, rounded, narrow and weeping types, each offering unique aesthetic and structural benefits.

Low-maintenance, hardy shrubs are ideal for all climates and soil types. Slow-growing varieties tend to have longer lifespans, reducing the need to replace them. Popular shrubs for each season include *Amelanchier lamarckii* in spring, *Rosa* spp. in summer, *Euonymus alatus* for autumn, and *Viburnum x bodnantense* for winter interest.

It's important to note that certain trees, such as alder, birch, ash and willow, can trigger asthma symptoms due to their pollen or volatile organic compounds (VOCs). Choosing the right trees and shrubs for your garden involves balancing aesthetics, function and long-term care. Fast-growing trees may offer quick coverage but may need replacing sooner than slower-growing species, which provide lasting value.

Once established, trees generally require less maintenance than shrubs. They need regular watering, mulching and occasional feeding in their early years and, once mature, only require periodic inspections and selective pruning. Larger trees may need professional care, especially for pruning or pest management. Shrubs, on the other hand, require more regular pruning, feeding and care, particularly if grown for flowers or formal shapes. .

Above Backlit by the sun, trees create dramatic shadows and dictate what type of plants need to be planted.

Thrifty trees

Silver birch

Betula spp.

Silver birches are loved for their white, sometimes pink or peeling, bark. They thrive in various soils, support over 300 insect species and offer seasonal beauty with catkins and autumn colour. Ideal for eco-friendly, thrifty gardens, they grow fast, serve as ornamental features and provide shelter for wildlife. Their spindly thin branches can be woven to make plant supports, for free.

Type deciduous
Height & spread
18 × 4m (60 × 13ft) in 20 years

Hornbeam

Carpinus betulus

Hornbeam is a hardy, versatile and cost-effective deciduous tree. It thrives in various soils, resists pests and requires minimal watering. Ideal for hedges (rather than costly fences or walls), topiary (rather than expensive sculpture), specimen trees and woodland plantings, it offers long lifespan, low-maintenance and provides organic matter to soil, making it a budget-friendly garden choice.

Type deciduous
Height & spread
11 × 6m (36 × 20ft) in 20 years

Maple

Acer spp.

Maple trees offer affordable, versatile options for gardens with over 130 species widely available at garden centres. They provide shade, stunning autumn colour and ornamental appeal. Hardy and low-maintenance maples tolerate various soil types and resist pests, so costly pesticides are not needed, making them an excellent budget-friendly and eco-conscious choice.

Type deciduous
Height & spread
varies, depending on variety

Choosing the right tree depends on size, shape and practical benefits. Compact, slow-growers suit small spaces, while larger species add structure to expansive areas. Tree form also impacts design, for example columnar trees fit smaller narrow areas, while weeping forms add softness and grace. Seasonal interest is also key. Native trees support a wide range of local wildlife, while soil and climate suitability ensure healthy growth. Consider, too, your maintenance demands and privacy needs. Low-maintenance trees fit better in smaller spaces, while hardier species like sweetgum and pine can handle high-traffic areas.

Ornamental Cherry

Prunus spp.

Ornamental cherry trees are beloved for their spring blossoms and versatility. Affordable and low-maintenance, they adapt to various soils, attract pollinators and enhance small gardens or urban spaces. Providing year-round beauty, they serve as focal points, create privacy and can increase property value without extensive upkeep. They're great multi-functional trees with spring blossom, autumn colours and decorative barks.

Type deciduous
Height & spread
8 × 6m (26 × 20ft) in 20 years

Hawthorn

Crataegus spp.

Hawthorn is a versatile, hardy and low-maintenance tree. It thrives in various conditions, attracts wildlife and offers year-round interest with flowers, berries and attractive foliage. Ideal for hedging, boundaries and wildlife gardens, hawthorn is budget-friendly, long-lived and adaptable to diverse soil and environmental conditions.

Type deciduous
Height & spread
8 × 8m (26 × 26ft) in 20 years

Holly

Ilex spp.

Holly is a budget-friendly, versatile evergreen plant known for its vibrant berries and foliage. It thrives in various soils, requires minimal maintenance and offers year-round structure. Holly is ideal for privacy screens, providing wildlife support (inviting both beneficial insects and natural predators), ground cover and as accent plants, making it a practical choice for diverse garden environments.

Type evergreen
Height & spread
6 × 3m (20 × 10ft) in 20 years

Thrifty shrubs

Barberry

Berberis spp.

Barberry is a budget-friendly, low-maintenance shrub available in various forms. It adapts to poor soils, requires minimal care and is drought-tolerant. Use it for hedges, ground cover, adding seasonal colour and attracting wildlife. Its dense, thorny foliage provides privacy and natural security, without the hefty costs of fencing or CCTV, while vibrant berries offer visual interest year-round.

Type deciduous or evergreen
Height & spread
1.5m × 1.5m (5 × 5ft) in 20 years

Pine

Pinus spp.

Pines are affordable, versatile, low-maintenance evergreens ideal for budget-conscious gardeners. Available as young saplings, they grow quickly in various soil types. Once established, they require minimal care and offer benefits like windbreaks, evergreen backdrops, wildlife habitat and erosion control. By growing dwarf pines on banks or slopes you can prevent soil erosion without having to pay to redirect stormwater.

Type evergreen
Height & spread
varies depending on variety

Witch hazel

Hamamelis spp.

Witch hazel is a hardy, low-maintenance shrub offering year-round interest with fragrant winter blooms and vibrant autumn foliage, often thriving for decades with minimal care. Resistant to pests and drought-tolerant, it flourishes in various conditions, making it a versatile, cost-wise choice as specimen plants, in borders and for wildlife support.

Type deciduous
Height & spread
6 × 5m (20 × 16ft) in 20 years

Shrubs are often referred to as the backbone to any garden. They can provide structure, shelter, colour, scent, form, shape, texture and movement and can be planted either in mass groupings or individually among herbaceous perennials, bulbs, ornamental grasses and even beneath trees. Many can be grown in containers, and a mix of evergreen, semi-evergreen and deciduous shrubs will create a rich, biodiverse garden. With the right choice, you can have continued interest in your garden all year. Shrubs can also be used to define spaces, add vertical interest, create natural screens and windbreaks, and support wildlife.

Viburnum

Viburnum spp.

Viburnum is a resilient shrub offering year-round interest, making it an excellent choice for thrifty gardeners. Affordable and adaptable, it requires minimal maintenance, is drought-tolerant and resistant to pests. With fragrant spring blooms, attractive foliage and colourful autumn berries, it enhances garden aesthetics and supports wildlife without significant investment.

Type deciduous and evergreen
Height & spread varies depending on variety

Hydrangea

Hydrangea spp.

Hydrangeas produce long-lasting blooms from early summer to autumn, providing visual impact. With various types and adaptability to light and soil conditions, they require minimal maintenance. Their striking colours vary according to soil pH. Hydrangeas are excellent for privacy screens, wildlife support and container gardening, making them the perfect frugal choice for all sizes of gardens. They come in many forms, such as mophead, panicle, oakleaf and climbing.

Type deciduous
Height & spread 3 × 3m (10 × 10ft) in 20 years, depending on variety

Rose

Rosa spp.

Once established, roses are low-maintenance, requiring only some care, like pruning. They thrive for years, reducing replanting costs. Available in various types, they adapt to different conditions. Roses bloom from early summer to autumn. They support wildlife, provide edible rose hips and petals and can be propagated cost-effectively. They come in many forms, such as hybrid tea, polyantha, floribunda, patio, climbing, damask, alba and rugosa.

Type deciduous
Height & spread varies depending on variety

Ornamentals

Ornamental plants are highly prized for their beauty and wide variety of colours, fruits, scents, textures, shapes, heights and spreads. Their flowers, colourful berries, leaves, interesting stems and bark and value for pollinators all make them essential for the thrifty gardener. With a good range of ornamentals, you can have year-round interest, especially if they have seasonal variation. This is important for the thrifty garden, as plants that change seasonally require fewer plants to create similar effects.

Choosing ornamentals

A diverse mix of ornamental plants, such as perennials, grasses, annuals, biennials, climbers, ferns, bulbs, corms, rhizomes and tubers, provides aesthetic appeal and a range of ecological and practical benefits for the thrifty gardener. While primarily valued for their beauty, these plants significantly enhance biodiversity, improve mental health and contribute to sustainable gardening practices. Many can be easily propagated, allowing you to fill your garden with free plants. Look out for plant sales at local events, community centres, gardening clubs or even the bargain section at nurseries. Shopping online is tempting but seeing the actual plants can prevent disappointment. Supermarkets often sell affordable ornamentals, and although these may not provide instant impact, thrifty gardening is about satisfaction in the long-term. Choosing dependable ornamental plants reduces the time spent on pest and disease management, allowing you to focus on timely garden tasks.

Thoughtfully selected ornamental plants can create habitats and food sources for wildlife, including insects, birds and small mammals, leading to higher insect biodiversity. Many ornamental species are excellent sources of nectar and pollen, supporting essential pollinators. For new and seasoned gardeners, ornamental plants can also create micro-climates, enhancing your garden's environment.

Annuals are appealing for their quick growth and flowering, providing instant gratification with a fast turnaround from planting to bloom. While preparing your garden beds and watching your

Above The topiary shrubs add shape and structure for 12 months of the year, while the wide range of plants, from perennials to climbers, shrubs to trees, add the colour, texture, shapes and scent.

perennials grow, annuals and biennials can fill gaps and offer immediate colour. Their seedheads will provide seeds for subsequent years, allowing for ongoing growth. In contrast, herbaceous perennials return year after year, providing reliability and reducing replacement costs over time. Their diverse flower shapes, colours and sizes add depth and visual interest. Once established, perennials require less maintenance, including watering and feeding, and many self-seed, leading to natural growth without the need for replanting – though careful management is needed to prevent overcrowding.

Climbers are often overlooked but can transform your garden by adding vertical interest. They can shelter wildlife while softening hard edges and covering unsightly structures. They're particularly beneficial in small gardens, on balconies or in urban spaces, maximizing vertical space without occupying valuable ground area. Climbers create layers and depth, drawing the eye upward and adding vibrancy and texture.

With their slender stems and leaves, ornamental grasses create movement that adds vitality to your garden. This movement contrasts nicely with static elements like hard landscaping or larger shrubs. Grasses can fill gaps or serve as striking standalone features.

Bulbs, corms, rhizomes and tubers can bring seasonal interest, often blooming early in spring, but many flower throughout the year. Once planted, bulbs require little care and return year after year, bringing colour when many plants are still dormant.

Finally, ferns offer versatility for shaded areas. They come in various colours, textures, shapes, heights and spreads, making them ideal for adding layers of interest to less sunny spots.

Thrifty perennials

Giant hyssop
Agastache spp.

Giant hyssop is a hardy, low-maintenance plant resistant to pests and diseases, requiring minimal care and water once established. Its long blooming season provides extended visual interest. Adaptable to various soils, it self-sows, reducing costs. *Agastache* attracts pollinators, offers vibrant colours and suits diverse garden styles.

Type deciduous perennial
Height & spread
90cm–1.2m × 60cm
(3–4ft × 2ft)

Monkshood or Wolfsbane
Aconitum spp.

Aconitum is a hardy perennial that requires minimal maintenance once established. It tolerates various soil types, is drought-tolerant and resists pests. With tall flower spikes, it adds vertical interest, blooms late in the season extending your garden's growing season and attracts pollinators, making it a valuable addition to your garden.

Type deciduous perennial
Height & spread
60cm–1.2m × 80cm
(2–4ft × 32in)

Coneflower
Echinacea spp.

A hardy perennial that returns each year, requiring minimal maintenance, it's drought-tolerant, pest-resistant and self-seeds, reducing costs. With vibrant blooms from mid-summer to autumn, it attracts pollinators and adds visual interest. Its root system also enhances soil health and structure.

Type deciduous perennial
Height & spread
90cm–1.2m × 30–45cm
(3–4ft × 12–18in)

Many gardeners will think of herbaceous perennials and ornamental grasses, especially when considering eco-friendly, water-wise and thrifty gardening. These will return every year, often getting bigger and better, especially when lifted and divided every three to five years to reinvigorate the plants and to make more for free. When seedheads and structure are left in autumn and winter, many look great speckled with frost or a light dusting of snow. Most herbaceous perennials and grasses need only to be cut back in the spring, before new growth emerges and deadheaded throughout the year to prolong flowering.

Cranesbill

Geranium spp.

Resilient perennials that return each year, saving costs on replanting, they require minimal maintenance, are drought-tolerant and resist pests and diseases. Their extended blooming period attracts pollinators, making them versatile for various garden settings, while their adaptability allows them to thrive in diverse conditions.

Type deciduous, semi-evergreen or evergreen perennial
Height & spread 30–90cm × 30–60cm (12–36in × 12–24in)

Sneezeweed

Helenium spp.

Helenium is an excellent choice for your garden. It is low-maintenance and doesn't require excessive watering or fertilization, helping to reduce ongoing garden maintenance costs. Once established, sneezeweed is moderately drought-tolerant and attracts a wide variety of pollinators. It is also relatively resistant to many common garden pests and diseases.

Type deciduous perennial
Height & spread 30cm–1.4m × 30–60cm (12inv5ft × 12–24in)

Knotweed

Persicaria spp.

Many *Persicaria* varieties produce flowers that bloom from summer to autumn, adding vibrant colour and interest when many other plants are past their prime. It can be used in mixed borders, woodland gardens and wildflower meadows. Some *Persicaria* species are excellent ground covers, helping to suppress weeds and prevent soil erosion.

Type deciduous perennial
Height & spread 15cm–1.5m × 50cm–1m (6in–5ft × 20in–5ft)

Thrifty grasses

Fountain grass
Pennisetum spp.

A low-maintenance, versatile ornamental grass that enhances garden aesthetics and provides seasonal interest. It propagates easily through division or seed, making it cost-effective. As a perennial, it returns yearly, quickly filling garden spaces and supporting wildlife while stabilizing soil and preventing erosion.

Type perennial grass
Height & spread
30cm–1.5m × 30cm–1.2m
(12in–5ft × 12in–4ft)

Feather grass
Stipa spp.

Stipa provides year-round interest. In spring and summer, it has soft, feathery plumes, while in the autumn, the foliage turns a golden hue, adding warm tones. It is highly versatile, suiting many garden styles, from modern and minimalist to cottage, prairie, Mediterranean and wildlife gardens. Perfect for softening edges in borders, creating focal points or as a filler plant to link different garden areas.

Type perennial grass
Height & spread
10cm–1m × 50cm–2.5m
(4–39in × 20in–8ft)

Maiden grass
Miscanthus spp.

Miscanthus has tall, graceful foliage and attractive flower plumes. Its variety of heights and colours complements different garden styles from modern to traditional. It provides lush green foliage in summer, dramatic plumes in autumn and interesting seedheads through winter. Taller varieties can be used to create natural screens; their dense growth helps shield unsightly views and adds structure to your borders.

Type perennial grass
Height & spread
80cm–4m × 90cm–1.5m
(32in–13ft × 36in–5ft)

Ornamental grasses offer a blend of beauty, versatility and ecological benefits. Their form, texture, movement and seasonal variation bring something other plants do not. Slender stems and leaves sway in the slightest breeze, creating an ever-changing display that can contrast to soften static elements.

They contribute to a healthy garden ecosystem, giving shelter and food to a range of wildlife. Dense clumps can be nesting sites, and seeds are an important food source during winter. Ornamental grasses work well in mixed schemes, filling in gaps, softening edges and combining well with different plant types.

Japanese forest grass

Hakonechloa spp.

Hakonechloa grass offers elegant cascading foliage, perfect for adding soft texture and movement to shaded gardens. Its arching leaves, often in bright greens or golds, create lush ground cover around borders and under trees. It is low-maintenance and tolerates partial to full shade, thriving in moist, well-drained soils. This grass turns warm shades of red and orange in autumn, enhancing year-round visual appeal with minimal upkeep.

Type perennial grass
Height & spread
10–50cm × 10–50cm
(4–20in × 4–20in)

Tufted hair grass

Deschampsia spp.

Deschampsia species bring airy elegance to gardens with their fine, feathery flowerheads that create a soft, cloud-like effect, especially when backlit. These grasses thrive in various soils and tolerate partial shade. Low-maintenance and resilient, they add structure and movement while attracting beneficial insects. In autumn, Deschampsia's foliage has warm tones. Ideal for naturalistic designs, they complement perennials and other grasses beautifully.

Typ perennial grass
Height & spread
30cm–1.5m × 15cm x 1m
(12in–5ft × 2–4ft)

Reed grass

Calamagrostis spp.

An affordable, low-maintenance perennial ideal for budget-conscious gardeners, its versatility provides year-round beauty with minimal care. Easy to propagate by division or seed, it adds structure and texture, stabilizes soil, complements various garden styles and attracts wildlife with its persistent seedheads.

Type perennial grass
Height & spread
60cm–1.2m × 60cm–1.2m
(2–4ft × 2–4ft)

Thrifty annuals and biennials

Cosmos

Cosmos spp.

This is an excellent choice for budget-conscious gardeners due to its affordability, easy care and versatility. Inexpensive seeds yield quick growth and vibrant blooms in various colours from pure white to deepest red and orange. Drought-tolerant and resistant to pests, Cosmos self-seeds, reducing replanting costs. Cosmos attracts pollinators and suits diverse garden border styles and containers.

Type predominantly deciduous annuals
Height & spread
45–90cm × 30cm–60cm
(18–36in × 12–24in)

Poppy

Papaver spp.

Poppies are a budget-friendly choice for gardeners, germinating in just one to two weeks, offering vibrant colours and unique forms with minimal investment. Their inexpensive seeds allow for large coverage and, once established, they self-seed, reducing costs. Hardy and low-maintenance, poppies thrive in various conditions, providing quick blooms and supporting pollinators while adding beauty to any garden space.

Type deciduous annual
Height & spread
30–90cm × 15–30cm
(12–36in × 6–12in)

Cornflower

Centaurea cyanus

Also called bachelor's button, this is an affordable, vibrant addition to your garden. Easy to grow from inexpensive seeds, it self-seeds, ensuring annual blooms without extra cost. Hardy and drought-tolerant, cornflowers attract beneficial insects, enhance biodiversity and serve as striking cut flowers, making them a versatile choice for budget-conscious gardeners.

Type annual or perennial
Height & spread
30–60cm × 30–60cm
(12–24in × 12–24in)

A few packets of annual and biennial seeds will not break the bank initially, and by collecting your own each year from the seedheads, you'll have a constant supply. They are quick growers; use them to fill your containers and borders while longer-term perennials, shrubs and trees are growing. Annuals and biennials can also complement and support the growth of other plants. For example, planting annuals around perennials can help suppress weeds and provide additional colour. Biennials, which often flower in late summer or early autumn, bridge seasonal gaps, adding colour and interest when other flowers have finished blooming.

Mexican sunflower

Tithonia rotundifolia

This is perfect for thrifty gardeners due to its affordability and rapid growth from seed. This vibrant, bright orange annual adds height, attracts pollinators, thrives in poor soil and requires minimal care. Its long-lasting blooms throughout summer and into autumn add a burst of colour, providing excellent value for a budget-friendly garden.

Type deciduous annual
Height & spread
1.8m × 45cm (6ft × 18in)

Foxglove

Digitalis spp.

Foxgloves are low-cost, easy-to-grow biennials/perennials that add height and colour to your garden. Once established, they self-seed and thrive in various conditions, especially dappled shade, with minimal maintenance. They attract pollinators and provide vibrant blooms, making them ideal for mixed plantings and naturalistic gardens.

Type deciduous biennial or short-lived evergreen
Height & spread
60cm–1.5m × 60cm–1.5m (24in–5ft × 24in–5ft)

Angelica

Angelica archangelica

For frugal gardeners wanting to add quick-growing height and structure to fill gaps, this is an ideal choice due to its affordability and striking presence. The architectural form, fragrant leaves and attractive flowers of this hardy biennial provide both ornamental beauty and pollinator support, and it self-seeds prolifically. With minimal maintenance and resilience in varying soil conditions, angelica thrives in cool, moist environments.

Type biennial or short-lived perennial
Height & spread
up to 2.5 × 2.5m (8 × 8ft)

Thrifty climbers

Clematis

Clematis spp.

Clematis is a diverse and beloved group of flowering plants known for stunning blooms in various colours and sizes. Their long lifespan makes them a cost-effective choice, as they continue to provide beauty year after year. Clematis is easy to propagate, offers vertical interest and attracts pollinators, enhancing garden value and biodiversity.

Type perennial climber or bushy shrub
Height & spread
1–7m × 1–7m (3–23ft × 3–23ft)

Wisteria

Wisteria spp.

This is a stunning, long-lived climber with fragrant, cascading flowers. Its longevity, minimal maintenance and rapid growth makes it a valuable investment. Once established, wisteria requires little care and quickly covers large areas, providing visual impact. It's also easy to propagate, making it budget-friendly for gardeners.

Type perennial, deciduous climber
Height & spread
3 × 3m (10 × 10ft)

Ivy

Hedera helix

Ivy, especially English ivy is a cost-effective, versatile plant ideal for covering large areas. Its hardy, evergreen foliage provides habitat for birds and insects, while its long lifespan ensures lasting value. Ivy also produces nectar-rich flowers and berries, supporting various wildlife and enhancing biodiversity in the garden.

Type hardy perennial climber or ground cover
Height & spread
20–30m × 4–8m
(66–100ft × 13–26ft)

Climbers can add vertical interest and beauty to your garden while providing shelter for wildlife and covering unsightly structures. They maximize limited space in small gardens or urban settings, create movement and sensory appeal, and serve as privacy screens and natural barriers. They can also impact your microclimate by insulating walls, keeping them cool in summer and warm in winter. Climbers like climbing roses and grapevines are low-maintenance and multifunctional once established. Mixing native hedging with climbers can replace costly fences, benefiting both wildlife and the environment.

Firethorn

Pyracantha spp.

A budget-friendly, hardy shrub offering year-round benefits, it's easy to source and ideal for creating hedges, for climbing walls or filling spaces. Its dense, thorny growth provides privacy and security, while spring flowers and colourful berries attract wildlife, making it a versatile and valuable garden addition.

Type hardy evergreen perennial climber, shrub or hedging
Height & spread
3–4m × 3–4m (10–13 × 10–13ft)

Chocolate vine

Akebia quinata

A great budget-friendly choice for thrifty gardeners, it's affordable, fast-growing and low-maintenance, providing quick coverage and unique fragrance. Its flowers attract pollinators, and it creates natural privacy screens. Versatile and visually appealing, it enhances gardens while supporting local wildlife and reducing screening costs.

Type semi-evergreen climber
Height & spread
10 × 2m (33 × 7ft)

Honeysuckle

Lonicera spp.

Honeysuckle is an excellent choice due to its affordability, rapid growth, sweetly scented flowers and low-maintenance needs. This versatile climber adds vibrant colour and fragrance while attracting pollinators. It can create natural privacy screens and cover unsightly structures, providing lasting beauty and wildlife support without high costs.

Type hardy, deciduous or evergreen climber
Height & spread
10 × 2m (33 × 7ft)

Thrifty ferns

Hart's tongue fern

Asplenium scolopendrium

Hart's tongue fern is an affordable, long-living, versatile evergreen fern that thrives in shade with minimal care. Once established, it requires little watering and is resilient to pests, reducing maintenance costs. As a native plant in many areas, it's well adapted to local conditions requiring fewer resources like fertilizers or soil amendments.

Type perennial, evergreen fern
Height & spread
30–60cm × 25–50cm
(12–24in × 10–20in)

Male fern

Dryopteris filix-mas

A classic deciduous fern that is affordable, hardy and low-maintenance. Thriving in various conditions, it requires minimal care once established, adapts to different soil types and is rarely affected by pests, reducing upkeep costs and efforts. It requires little more than occasional watering during extended dry spells and benefits from a mulch of organic matter in the spring to maintain soil moisture and promote growth.

Type perennial, deciduous fern
Height & spread
1–1.5m × 50cm–1m
(3–5ft × 20in–3ft)

Japanese lace fern

Polystichum polyblepharum

A beautiful, evergreen addition to your garden that is both cost-effective and easy to maintain. Known for its glossy, dark green fronds with a distinctive 'tasselled' appearance as new growth emerges, this fern provides year-round interest with minimal care. It is a long-lived perennial and thrives in partial to full shade.

Type perennial, evergreen fern
Height & spread
60–90cm × 60–90cm
(24–36in × 24–36in)

Ferns are a fantastic option for thrifty gardeners due to their resilience, minimal maintenance needs and versatility. These hardy plants thrive in various conditions, making them suitable for shady areas where many other plants struggle. Once established, ferns require little watering and no fertilization, which saves on gardening costs. Their lush foliage adds texture and visual interest to the garden without requiring frequent replacement. Many ferns can be easily propagated through division or spores, allowing gardeners to expand their collection at no extra cost. Ferns also support local wildlife.

Hard fern
Blechnum spicant

Also known as the deer fern, this is an excellent plant due to its resilience, versatility and ease of propagation. It is named for its tough, leathery fronds that can withstand cold winters, wet soils and shaded areas. It is also naturally tolerant of acidic soils and only requires watering during extended dry spells.

Type perennial evergreen fern
Height & spread
45–60cm × 45–90cm (18–24in × 18–36in)

Sword fern
Polystichum munitum

A cost-effective, hardy plant perfect for thrifty gardeners. It thrives in various soil types and light conditions, requiring minimal care once established. Its lush foliage provides year-round greenery, and supports local wildlife, making it a valuable, low-maintenance addition to any landscape.

Type perennial evergreen fern
Height & spread
90cm × 1.2m (3 × 4ft)

Common polypody fern
Polypodium vulgare

Native to Great Britain, this affordable hardy fern thrives in various conditions, including damp or dry shade and rocky soils, requiring minimal maintenance. This resilient plant adds lush greenery to gardens while supporting biodiversity, making it a practical choice for low-cost, eco-friendly gardening.

Type perennial evergreen fern
Height & spread
30cm × 1m (12 × 39in)

Thrifty bulbs, corms, rhizomes and tubers

Lily
Lilium spp.

A budget-friendly choice, offering beauty, durability and low-maintenance, these affordable bulbs yield stunning blooms year after year, making them a cost-effective investment. Once established, lilies require minimal care, thriving in well-drained soil with moderate watering, providing long-lasting colour and elegance in the garden. Most grow in sun but martagon lilies can also be grown in dappled shade.

Type perennial bulb
Height & spread
30cm–1.8m × 15–30cm
(12in–6ft × 6–12in)

Tulip
Tulipa spp.

Tulips are an excellent budget-friendly option for spring displays. These affordable bulbs allow for substantial planting without significant investment. Once planted, they can bloom year after year, providing great value, but to ensure long life and repeated flowering, it's best to lift the bulbs. Tulips are fairly low-maintenance, requiring only a sunny spot and well-drained soil, minimal watering and pest resistance.

Type perennial bulb
Height & spread
10–70cm × 10–15cm
(4–27in × 4–6in)

Allium
Allium spp.

Alliums, like *Allium giganteum* and *Allium hollandicum*, are budget-friendly and easy to propagate, offering long-term savings. They thrive with minimal care, requiring well-drained soil and full sun. As perennials, they return annually, providing striking globe-like flowers that add drama to your garden without constant replacement.

Type perennial bulb
Height & spread
15cm–1.5m × 10cm–30cm
(6in–5ft × 4–12in)

These plants offer great value, visual impact and ecological benefits. They are generally inexpensive (many can be bought in bulk, some in mixed bags) and provide vibrant blooms or foliage year after year, reducing the need for replanting. Low-maintenance, they require minimal care once established. Many bulbs, such as daffodils, and tubers, such as dahlia, also multiply over time, allowing you to propagate your collections without additional costs. They can also fill gaps in your garden and attract pollinators. Their wide variety ensures you can choose options that suit your aesthetic preferences and local conditions.

Crocus

Crocus spp.

These corms are economical and can be purchased in bulk, making them ideal for impactful displays. They return annually, naturalizing and multiplying over time for long-term value. Hardy and low-maintenance, they thrive in well-drained soil, tolerate drought and are resilient to pests, providing early spring colour in your garden.

Type perennial corm
Height & spread
7–12cm × 7–12cm (3–5in × 3–5in)

Iris

Iris spp.

Irises can be bulbs or rhizomes and are a budget-friendly choice due to their stunning blooms and low-maintenance. These hardy perennials, with their grass-like foliage and vibrant colours and textures, thrive in various soil types and return year after year. Once established, irises require minimal care. With rhizomes, sections can be cut off with a knife and replanted elsewhere in your garden.

Type rhizome or perennial bulb
Height & spread
10cm–1.2m × 5cm–2m (4in–4ft × 2in–7ft)

Dahlia

Dahlia spp.

Dahlias tubers are inexpensive and can be bought in bulk. These perennials bloom year after year when properly stored over winter, offering great value. Easy to grow in well-drained soil, they require regular watering and feeding and are generally hardy with manageable pest issues. Coming in all shapes and sizes, they are perfect for the thrifty gardener.

Type perennial tuber
Height & spread
35cm–1.2m × 30–80cm (15in–4ft × 12–32in)

Edibles

Edible plants, such as vegetables (including microgreens), fruits, herbs and edimentals, can transform your garden into a productive space, providing fresh produce, promoting sustainability and fostering a connection to nature and seasonality. Growing edible plants allows you to access fresh, nutrient-rich produce. Home-grown fruits, vegetables and herbs are often more flavourful and nutritious than store-bought options, as they can be harvested at peak ripeness and consumed shortly after picking. For example, tomatoes harvested at peak ripeness contain more lycopene – a potent antioxidant – than those picked green and ripened during transport.

Above Cut-and-come-again lettuces can be grown in recycled wooden or plastic crates, providing months of delicious, nutritious food for the price of a packet of seeds.

Choosing edibles

Growing edible plants can lead to significant cost savings. By growing your own food, you can reduce grocery bills, especially for expensive or speciality produce. Additionally, producing food at home reduces dependence on commercially grown produce, which can be subject to price fluctuations. Therefore, significant savings can be made annually on food expenses by growing your own edibles.

Edible gardening promotes sustainability by reducing the carbon footprint associated with food production and transportation. Gardens require fewer resources, such as water and synthetic fertilizers, than large-scale commercial agriculture. Moreover, organic gardening practices can further enhance sustainability by eliminating use of harmful pesticides and chemicals.

Also, integrating edible plants into your garden will increase biodiversity, which is crucial for your garden's ecosystem health. A diverse garden supports various organisms, including beneficial insects, birds and soil microbes. This biodiversity can lead to more resilient and productive ecosystems.

Edible gardening can foster a sense of community and social interaction. Community gardens or just sharing what you've grown over the garden fence with neighbours will lead to collaboration, knowledge-sharing and community engagement opportunities.

So, to maximize the benefits of edible plants in your garden and to help supplement diets and ensure a steady supply of nutritious food, consider these eight practical tips:

1. **Choose a variety of plants** Incorporate a mix of fruits, vegetables, herbs, fungi and edible flowers to ensure a diverse and continuous harvest throughout the growing season.

2. **Practise crop rotation** Rotate crops each year to prevent soil depletion and reduce the risk of pests and diseases.

3. **Use companion planting** Combine complementary species to enhance growth, deter pests and improve soil health. For example, basil planted alongside tomatoes can improve flavour and repel insects.

4. **Follow organic practices** Avoid synthetic chemicals and use organic methods such as composting, mulching and natural pest control to maintain soil health and protect beneficial organisms.

5. **Avoid using peat** and only use peat-free composts if you need to buy it, or make your own compost (see pages 34–37).

6. **Harvest regularly** This encourages continuous production and prevents plants from becoming overgrown or stressed.

7. **Plan for season extension** You can use cold frames, row covers and indoor gardening to extend the growing season to maximize your harvest.

8. **Engage with your community** Participate in community gardening projects and share excess produce with neighbours to build social connections and promote local food networks.

Edible plants are a valuable addition to any garden, offering many benefits beyond their culinary uses. They contribute to nutritional health, economic savings, environmental sustainability, biodiversity and your, as well as your community, wellbeing.

Thrifty veg

Carrot
Daucus carota subsp. sativus

Carrots require minimal space and care, making them easy to grow in various conditions. With a single packet of seeds, you can harvest a substantial crop, providing excellent value for your investment. Harvested carrots can also be stored in a cool, dark place for several months. Look for: 'Nantes 2', 'Chantenay Red Core' and 'Little Finger'.

Type biennial
Height & spread
30–60cm × 10cm (12–24in × 4in)

Courgette
Cucurbita pepo

Courgettes are an excellent option for budget-conscious gardeners due to their low-cost seeds and high productivity. They thrive in warm, sunny conditions and grow rapidly with little maintenance. A few courgette plants can deliver a bountiful harvest, ensuring you get great value from your gardening efforts. Look for: 'Defender', 'Black Beauty' and 'Soleil'.

Type annual
Height & spread
45–90cm (19–36in)

Squash
Cucurbita spp.

Squashes are grown from seeds, which can be sown directly into the soil or started indoors for an earlier harvest. They generally require warm soil temperatures and plenty of space due to their sprawling nature. Pick summer squashes when young and tender, while winter squashes are left to mature fully on the vine before harvesting. Look for: 'Butternut Waltham', 'Patty Pan' and 'Sweet Dumpling'.

Type annual
Height & spread
60–90cm × 4.5m
(24–36in × 15ft)

Vegetables can provide excellent value with their high yields from minimal seed and need for minimal care, thriving in various soil types and conditions. Vegetable seeds are inexpensive and often sold in bulk or mixed packets, or you can leave some plants to flower to set seed for collection. When it comes to growing vegetables, consider companion planting. For example, carrots, whose deep roots can help break up soil and improve its structure, grow well alongside onions and lettuce.

Radish

Raphanus sativus

Radishes are an excellent choice due to their rapid growth and high yield. They germinate quickly, allowing for a fast harvest within weeks. Low-cost seeds and minimal space requirements make them ideal for small gardens and vegetable container gardening. Additionally, radishes add a peppery flavour to dishes and are nutritious. Look for: 'Caro', 'French Breakfast' and 'Rainbow Mix'.

Type annual
Height & spread
60–90cm × 30–60cm
(24–36in × 12–24in)

Rhubarb

Rheum rhabarbarum

Rhubarb is a fantastic choice because it's a hardy perennial that thrives with minimal care, returning year after year. Its tart stalks have many culinary uses, from pies to jams. Once established, rhubarb requires little maintenance, providing a bountiful harvest and excellent value over time. Look for: 'Strawberry', 'Victoria' and 'Red Champagne'.

Type perennial
Height & spread
60–90cm × 1–1.2m
(24–36in; 3–4ft)

Lettuce

Lactuca sativa

Growing lettuce is beneficial due to its fast growth and high yield. Lettuce can be sown directly in the garden or containers, requiring minimal space. It thrives in a variety of conditions and can be harvested multiple times throughout the season, providing fresh greens for salads and sandwiches. Cut-and-come-again lettuce can provide a continuous harvest.

Type annual
Height & spread
15–30cm × 15–30cm
(6–12in × 6–12in)

Thrifty fruit

Apple tree

Malus spp.

While the initial cost of purchasing apple tree saplings might be higher than seeds or seedlings, the long-term benefits outweigh the cost. Once established, apple trees typically provide years of harvest, making them a worthwhile investment. While apple trees require some care, such as pruning, pest control and proper watering, they are generally less labour-intensive than annual plants.

Type deciduous, perennial tree
Height & spread
4.5 × 4.5m (15 × 15ft)

Pear tree

Pyrus communis

Pears can be expensive to buy, yet they are relatively low-maintenance to grow, making them ideal for busy gardeners. They produce abundant, sweet fruit and are attractive landscape features, offering beautiful spring blossoms and vibrant autumn foliage. Growing pears can also contribute to local biodiversity, supporting pollinators and wildlife in your garden.

Type deciduous, perennial tree
Height & spread
3.5–12m × 3–4m
(12–40ft × 10–13ft)

Cherry tree

Prunus spp.

Cherries can be very expensive to buy, so growing them yourself is both rewarding and will save you a lot of money in the long term. Not only will you have stunning spring blossoms but, once established, a mature cherry tree can produce up to 7,000 cherries. Keep an eye out for birds, however, as they, too, love cherries!

Type deciduous,
perennial tree
Height & spread
6–8m × 5m (20–26ft × 16ft)

For fresh, organic fruit, free from pesticides and chemicals, grow your own. When choosing what to grow, consider these key factors: plot size – trees like apple or pear require space, though smaller bushes or espaliered or stepover trees suit compact areas. High-yield plants like raspberries produce regularly; others – grapes and peaches – bear seasonally. Check climate compatibility, as some fruits need specific temperature ranges. Soil quality should match the fruit's needs, and sunlight is crucial for most fruits to ripen fully. Some fruits like apples and blackberries need regular pruning. Finally, some plants need cross-pollinators to bear fruit.

Strawberry

Fragaria spp.

Delicious strawberries are relatively easy to cultivate and produce abundant yields in a small space. Strawberries thrive in various conditions and can be grown in pots and containers, making them an ideal choice for both novice and experienced gardeners. Also consider growing them in hanging baskets or fabric wall pockets for their ornamental flowers and red fruits. They are easily propagated from runners.

Type short-lived perennial
Height & spread
30 × 60cm (12 × 24in)

Raspberry

Rubus idaeus

Growing raspberries is a cost-effective choice for gardeners, as these perennials produce high yields year after year with minimal investment. Once established, they require little maintenance and can yield a significant amount of fruit, reducing the need to purchase expensive store-bought berries while ensuring fresh, delicious produce at home. Look for both summer- and autumn-fruiting varieties.

Type perennial bush
Height & spread
1.8 × 2m (6 × 7ft)

Blueberry

Vaccinium corymbosum

Growing blueberries support local ecosystems by attracting pollinators like bees and beneficial insects. Their deep roots enhance soil structure and prevent erosion, while organic cultivation reduces reliance on chemical pesticides. Blueberries also provide habitat for wildlife, promoting biodiversity and contributing to a healthier environment. They also have stunning autumn colours and work in containers or mixed borders as decorative shrubs.

Type perennial bush
Height & spread
1.5 × 1.5m (5ft × 5ft)

Thrifty herbs

Basil

Ocimum basilicum

A popular herb with aromatic leaves used in cooking, particularly in Italian cuisine, basil thrives in warm, sunny conditions. It is easy to grow from seeds or cuttings and needs warm temperatures to germinate. Look for 'Genovese', 'Purple Ruffles' and 'Lemon'.

Type half-hardy annual
Height and spread
30 × 30cm (12 × 12in)

Mint

Mentha spp.

Mint is a versatile herb with a refreshing flavour. It can be used in teas, desserts and savoury dishes. It is easily propagated from cuttings or by dividing root clumps. Mint can be invasive, so it is good that it grows well in containers to prevent spreading. Look for 'Peppermint', 'Spearmint', and 'Chocolate'.

Type hardy perennial
Height and spread
1 × 1m (3 × 3ft)

Chives

Allium schoenoprasum

A mild onion-flavoured herb used in salads, soups and as a garnish, chives also have attractive purple flowers. They can be propagated by dividing clumps or grown from seeds. They tolerate a range of soil conditions. Look for 'Common', 'Garlic' and 'Fine Leaf'.

Type hardy perennial
Height and spread
30 × 20cm (12 × 8in)

Herb seeds or seedlings are cost-effective, often inexpensive and can be grown from kitchen scraps or saved seeds, further reducing costs. Many herbs are prolific, providing a substantial harvest throughout the growing season. Herb plants can thrive in small spaces, containers or indoors, making them ideal for limited areas. Most herbs are hardy and require minimal care, needing less water and fertilizer than many other plants. Additionally, herbs can serve as companion plants, repelling pests and attracting beneficial insects, which reduces the need for chemical pesticides and enhances overall garden health.

Rosemary

Rosmarinus officinalis

An aromatic herb with needle-like leaves used in cooking and grown as a decorative plant, rosemary has a distinctive, pine-like-floral flavour. It can be grown from seeds or cuttings. It prefers full sun and well-drained soil. Look for 'Tuscan Blue', 'Arp' and 'Prostratus'.

Type hardy evergreen perennial
Height and spread
1.5 × 1.5m (5 × 5ft)

Thyme

Thymus vulgaris

A hardy herb with a strong, earthy flavour, thyme is used in various cuisines and is also an attractive ground cover to suppress weeds and lock in moisture. It is easily grown from seeds or cuttings. Prefers well-drained soil and sunny conditions. Look for 'Common', 'Lemon' and 'Wild'.

Type hardy, evergreen perennial
Height and spread
30 × 20cm (12 × 8in)

Coriander

Coriandrum sativum

Both the leaves and seeds are used in cooking, making it a great, cost-effective herb. It has a bright, fresh flavour. It is grown from seeds. Prefers cooler weather and can be harvested multiple times. Look for 'Santo', 'Confetti' and 'Calypso'.

Type hardy annual
Height and spread
50 × 25cm (20 × 10in)

Thrifty edimentals

Jerusalem artichoke

Helianthus tuberosus

This plant is a species of sunflower native to North America, known for its edible tubers. It is hardy and adaptable, thriving in various soil types and conditions. It can also tolerate drought and is relatively low-maintenance. Its tall, attractive flowers attract pollinators like bees and butterflies, making it a cost-effective, dual-purpose edimental.

Type hardy perennial
Height & spread
1.2–3m × 60cm–1m
(4–10ft × 2–3ft

Chard

Beta vulgaris

This leafy green is not only nutritious but also has visually appealing colourful stems and leaves. Chard pairs well with flowering plants like marigolds and herbs, which can deter pests and enhance biodiversity. You can either sow chard seeds directly into the soil or transplant seedlings. By regularly harvesting the leaves to promote new growth, you'll keep your chard productive throughout the season.

Type biennial
Height & spread
50 × 50cm (20 × 20in)

Nasturtium

Tropaeolum majus

Both the leaves and flowers are edible, with a peppery flavour. It adds vibrant colour to gardens and attracts beneficial insects. Nasturtium seeds are generally inexpensive and often available in bulk and can be collected after flowering. A small seed investment can lead to many plants, providing significant value for your money.

Type annual or perennial
Height & spread
30cm–1.5m × 45cm–1.5m
(12in–5ft × 18in–5ft)

Edimentals combine the terms 'edible' and 'ornamental', and are aesthetically pleasing with edible leaves, flowers, fruits or roots. As such they are ideal if you want to maximize space and resources. Common examples include nasturtium (*Tropaeolum majus*), chard (*Beta vulgaris*), lavender (*Lavandula* spp.) and perilla (*Perilla frutescens*). Growing edimentals allows you to produce food in a visually appealing way, while attracting beneficial insects and pollinators. This helps with biodiversity and creates a balanced ecosystem; natural predators do the work for you, without the cost of pesticides.

Pot marigold

Calendula officinalis

Known for its bright orange and yellow flowers, calendula petals are edible and often used in salads and as a garnish. A single packet of seeds can yield many plants, providing excellent value for money. Calendula is known for its ability to self-seed. Once established, it can drop seeds that will germinate the following season, reducing the need for replanting and saving you the cost of new seeds.

Type hardy annual
Height & spread
50 × 50cm (20 × 20in)

Dandelion

Taraxacum officinale

Dandelions are excellent edimentals due to their versatility and nutritional value. Their leaves are rich in vitamins A, C and K, as well as minerals like iron and calcium, making them a healthy addition to salads and smoothies, and their roots have medicinal properties, often used in detoxifying teas. Dandelions are low-maintenance and resilient.

Type hardy perennial
Height & spread
5–50cm × 15–30cm (2–20in × 6–12in)

Borage

Borago officinalis

The leaves and flowers are edible, and the plant produces beautiful star-shaped blue flowers, making it a stunning addition to any garden or drink. This hardy herb attracts pollinators like bees, enhancing biodiversity. It also contributes to improved soil health and suppresses weeds, making it a valuable companion plant.

Type hardy annual
Height & spread
70 × 50cm (27 × 20in)

CARING FOR YOUR GARDEN

Observing your garden, designing your outdoor space, creating growing areas and introducing plants and wildlife is only the beginning of your gardening journey. With the right care and attention, your garden will grow. You'll need to discover what ongoing care and maintenance it will need and how much attention will be required while also expanding your garden and gardening knowledge. It is important to always maintain an eco-friendly, sustainable garden that has been approached with a thrifty mindset.

Throughout this book, I've highlighted key plants you could grow, but understanding the basics to good planting will ensure that your plants get off to a roaring start and will continue to grow. With burgeoning life, fresh green shoots and woody stems, it's essential to know the basics of pruning, why watering, feeding and mulching are vital to a healthy garden and why, with observing and working with nature and the seasons, you'll get to grips with seasonality and see your garden with fresh eyes. You will create a garden that has interest for 12 months of the year, but there will be times when you can sit back and enjoy the fruits of your labour.

I know it can be difficult to step outside when it's lashing with rain or there's a chill in the air, but, remember, gardening will give you a physical workout. I remember someone saying to me there is no such thing as bad weather, just bad clothing. This is so true. After 20 minutes of hard gardening, such as raking thatch from a lawn, digging over a border or turning your compost, you'll have warmed up and probably forgotten about the weather.

To maintain your garden, you'll have to put in a lot of work. But, trust me, once you get the gardening and propagation bug, you'll wonder how you lived without them. Gardening can ground us in the here and now, yet we gardeners are constantly planning for the future. Look forward to your bounties, to your colourful pots, containers and borders and relish every moment.

Plants for free

Growing plants for free through propagation (i.e. creating new plants from existing ones) provides several benefits. First, it eliminates the need to buy new plants, as you can grow many from cuttings, seeds or division, making it an economical option. Secondly, it's a sustainable practice, reducing waste and minimizing the environmental impact of purchasing mass-produced plants with their heavy resource use in terms of water, fertilizers, manpower and transport. It allows you to share plants with friends, create a more personalized garden and preserve heirloom varieties. Propagation also gives you control over the health of your plants, as you can select the strongest specimens to reproduce, resulting in a vibrant, flourishing garden at no extra cost.

There are various methods of propagation, and each is suited to different plant types, but they generally fall into two categories: sexual (using seeds) and asexual (using vegetative parts like cuttings, divisions or layering).

Above Coir, knitted or terracotta pots, along with peat-free expandable pellets, are all perfect for growing plants.

Sexual propagation

This involves growing plants from seeds, the most natural form of plant reproduction. This method is often used for annuals, vegetables, herbs and flowers, as well as perennials, trees and shrubs. Many gardeners enjoy the process of starting plants from seed because it provides the full experience of nurturing a plant from the very beginning of its life.

Seeds for a large range of plant types are widely available to buy inexpensively, but collecting and saving seeds from your garden makes propagation cost-free. However, growing from seed requires patience. Not all plants germinate quickly and some require specific conditions, such as cold stratification or soaking. Additionally, plants grown from seed may not always be identical to the parent plant, particularly in the case of hybrids.

Despite these challenges, sexual propagation is an excellent way to introduce biodiversity to your garden, as seed-grown plants can have slight genetic variations, sometimes resulting in stronger plants with better resistance to pests and diseases.

Asexual propagation

Asexual or vegetative propagation involves creating new plants from parts of an existing plant, such as from stems, roots, leaves or even bulbs and tubers. The most common methods include cuttings, division, layering and grafting. Asexual propagation produces clones of the parent plant, meaning the offspring will be genetically identical. This is particularly useful if you have a plant with desirable traits – such as a beautiful flower colour or exceptional hardiness – that you want to reproduce exactly.

Taking cuttings involves taking a small section of a plant, usually a stem or leaf, and encouraging it to grow roots. Plants like lavender, rosemary and geraniums are often propagated through

Above Dividing a plant is one of the simplest methods of propagation. Use a knife, your hands or a spade, depending on the root type.

cuttings. Rooting hormone compound can sometimes be used to encourage faster root development, but this isn't always necessary.

Division involves splitting an established plant into two or more parts, each of which can be replanted. This works well for hostas, daylilies and many herbaceous perennials. It is typically done during the dormant season in autumn or early spring to reduce stress on the plant.

Layering is when part of the plant is bent to the ground and covered with soil, and eventually forms roots. Once rooted, the new plant can be separated from the parent. This method is common for plants like strawberries, blackberries and some shrubs.

Grafting involves attaching a piece of one plant to another to improve fruit production or increase hardiness. Fruit trees, particularly apples and cherries, are often grafted.

Agapanthus
10/10/24

Collecting seeds

Collecting seeds is a smart, thrifty approach because it turns plants into ongoing investments. Start by identifying healthy, vigorous plants with desirable traits. Wait for seeds to fully mature before collecting. This is usually when flowers fade, seed pods dry, or fruits have fully ripened or are mature. Seeds are best stored in paper bags or envelopes (they can rot in plastic), once the chaff (husk) has been removed. Make sure you label them properly, and use them within a year of collection. Storing your packets of seeds in an airtight container at the back of the fridge can significantly prolong their life. To check whether or not your refrigerated collected seeds are viable, drop them into a glass of water. Those that sink are likely viable, while those that float may not germinate.

Ingredients

+ Scissors or secateurs
+ Seedhead, seed pod/capsule or fruit
+ Paper bag or envelope and pencil
+ Tweezers
+ Air-tight plastic container with lid
+ Dry rice or a silica gel bag (recycled from delivery packages)

Opposite Dried agapanthus flower heads contain black seeds that can be collected, stored or sown straight away.

1.

Wait for a still, dry day to harvest your seeds. Have ready the paper bag or envelope and write the name of the plant and the date you collected them on it.

2.

Depending on the nature of the plant, cut a stem between 20–30cm (8–12in) in length, remove a seed pod/capsule or pick a fully ripe fruit (see step 5 below). Insert the seedhead or pod into the envelope or bag.

3.

Leave in the bag for a few days for seeds to loosen from the seedhead, capsule or pod. You can shake it gently to facilitate this. Open the bag and remove the chaff (the husk surrounding the seed), the stem and other detritus, using tweezers or by gently blowing, leaving just the seed/s.

4.

Seal the envelope or bag and place in an air-tight container with 1 tbsp of dried rice or a recycled silica gel bag to absorb any unwanted moisture and protect the seeds. Cover with the lid and place at the back of your fridge until ready to use.

5.

For fruits, remove the seeds by using your fingers or tweezers and place the seeds onto a piece of kitchen towel to dry. Once dry, place them inside an envelope or bag and follow the above instructions.

Sowing seeds

Sowing seeds is an easy and rewarding way to start your garden because it's accessible to all, even for beginners. With just soil, water and sunlight, you can watch a tiny seed transform into a thriving plant. It's a low-cost method that provides many plants from a collection of seeds, making it budget-friendly too. The process builds patience and connection to the natural cycle, as you nurture each stage of growth. When seedlings finally mature, there's immense satisfaction in knowing you've grown them from scratch, enriching your garden with life and colour in a deeply personal way.

Ingredients

+ Seed tray with drainage holes or recycled clear plastic fruit punnet with lid or margarine tub
+ 9–10cm (3½–4in) pots
+ Saved seeds
+ Peat-free multi-purpose compost and horticultural grit
+ Plant label and pencil

1.

Fill the seed tray (or one of the pots) with a 50:50 mix of peat-free compost and horticultural grit. Sit the tray or pot into a reservoir of water and wait until the soil surface looks damp and shiny.

2.

Scatter the seeds over the surface of the soil. Do your best to leave space between each one; this can be tricky with fine seeds. Use the back of your hand to gently press down on the seeds to ensure they are in direct contact with the soil. Cover with a layer of horticultural grit and label.

3.

Place in a warm, bright spot (around 20°C/70°F) in indirect sunlight. Check the soil often. Germination rates vary depending on the species.

4.

Once you have seedlings with established roots and one set of true leaves (i.e. those that emerge after the initial cotyledons, or seed leaves, and resemble those of the parent plant), transplant each one into its own 9cm (3½in) pot. To do this, fill the pot with compost and make a hole in the centre before carefully lifting each seedling from the seed tray and into its own pot. Use a pencil or chopstick to help you and always hold seedlings by their leaves, never their stems.

5.

Continue to care for the plant as you would any other young plant, gradually acclimatizing it to outdoor conditions if needed.

Planting depths for seeds

<1.5cm (½in) deep – artichoke, beetroot, broccoli, Brussel sprouts, cabbage, carrot, cauliflower, celery, kale, kohlrabi, leek, lettuce, melon, parsnip, pepper, radish

2–2.5cm (1–1¼in) deep – cucumber, okra, pea, sweetcorn

2.5–4cm (1–1¾in) deep – asparagus, climbing bean, onion

5cm (2in)+ deep – broad bean, potato

Sowing large seeds

To sow large seeds such as pot marigold, broad bean, sunflower or sweet pea, insert each one into the soil up to your first knuckle and cover with soil.

Stem cuttings

Stem cuttings are a simple and effective way to propagate plants vegetatively, allowing gardeners to produce new plants identical to the parent. This method is often faster and less expensive than growing from seed. New roots develop by cutting a healthy piece of a plant's stem, rooting it in water or soil, and providing the right conditions. This technique works well for many shrubs, perennials and houseplants. It's a popular choice because it allows for preserving desirable traits, such as flower colour or growth habit, while also expanding your garden with minimal resources.

Ingredients

+ Several 10–15cm (4–6in) pieces of plant stems
+ Pruning shears, secateurs, kitchen scissors or a knife
+ Hormone-rooting powder, gel or turmeric (optional)
+ 9–10cm (3½–4in) terracotta pot (recycled plastic is fine, such as clear plastic fruit punnets with lids)
+ Peat-free or sandy compost, perlite or horticultural grit
+ Pen
+ Plant label
+ Clear plastic bag (or propagator or handmade cold frame)

1.
Select a healthy, non-flowering stem from a disease-free parent plant to increase the chances of successful rooting. Use sharp clean pruning shears, secateurs, kitchen scissors or a knife to take a 10–15cm (4–6in) cutting just below a node (where a leaf attaches to the stem) with a few leaves at the top.

2.
Strip off the lower leaves, leaving two or three leaves at the top to reduce water loss.

3.
If you wish, dip the cut end of the stem into rooting powder, gel or turmeric. This can help stimulate root growth, especially for woody plants or more challenging species.

4.
Fill a 9–10cm (3½–4in) pot, ideally terracotta but plastic will do, with a mix (1:4) of perlite and peat-free or sandy compost, water lightly and add a label. Terracotta pots, being a natural material, are porous allowing for excellent air circulation and drainage, preventing root rot and promoting healthy root development.

5.
With your finger or a pencil, make a small hole in the soil around the edge of the pot and insert the stem cutting about 3–5cm (1¼–2in) deep, enough to cover the bottom node then water to settle the soil. Remember to add a plant label using an indelible ink pen.

6.
To create a humid environment, cover the pot with a clear plastic bag, ensuring the bag doesn't touch the cutting (or place the lid on the punnet if you can do so without touching the cutting). Place in a warm, bright spot (around 20°C/70°F) with indirect sunlight. A propagator or a cold frame are ideal. Maintain consistent moisture and warmth. Open or lift off the plastic cover occasionally to let in fresh air and reduce condensation.

7.
Rooting time varies depending on the plant species, but once established, transplant into an individual larger pot with peat-free potting compost. Continue to care for the plant as you would any other young plant, gradually acclimatizing it to outdoor conditions if needed.

Keep blades clean

Disinfect your blades between cuttings to prevent the spread of disease. Wipe them down with a mix of 1 part bleach to 10 parts warm water.

Put whole pot into a bag

Take a large plastic bag, insert the pot with soil and cuttings into the bag. Twist the top, but before tying with a piece of string, blow into the bag to enrich the carbon dioxide content.

Leaf cuttings

Leaf cuttings are a simple and cost-effective way to propagate plants, especially for species that do not readily grow from seeds or stem cuttings, such as *Eucomis* spp. and *Begonia rex* hybrids. By using a healthy leaf, you can create new plants identical to the parent. This method also works well for plants like succulents and African violets. Leaf cuttings allow you to preserve desirable traits, such as unique foliage patterns or colours, while ensuring successful growth through a relatively low-effort process that requires minimal equipment.

Ingredients

+ Leaf cutting
+ Pair of scissors or a knife
+ Rubbing alcohol or a mix of 1 part bleach to 10 parts warm water to disinfect your blades between taking cuttings
+ 9–10cm (3½ –4in) terracotta pot (recycled plastic is fine, such as plastic fruit punnets)
+ Peat-free multi-purpose compost, perlite or horticultural grit
+ Pen and plant label
+ Clear plastic bag (or propagator or handmade cold frame)

1.

Select a healthy, disease-free leaf from the parent plant, avoiding damaged or yellowing leaves, as they are less likely to root successfully.

2.

Use sterilized sharp, clean scissors or a knife to make the cut. For plants like begonias or African violets, cut the leaf stem (petiole) about 3–5cm (1¼ –2in) below the leaf. For succulents, cut the entire leaf at the base and leave for 1–2 days to callus or heal over – soft tissue forms over the cut end, leading to healing. Clean blades (see pages 52, 184–5) if cutting more than one leaf.

3.

Fill a 9cm (3½ in) pot with a mix (50:50) of horticultural grit and peat-free compost and water to lightly moisten and add a label. Insert the leaf's petiole (the area of a leaf that connects the leaf blade to the stem) into the soil or lay leaf sections flat, vein side down, ensuring the cut edges make contact with the soil. For succulents, simply place the leaf's base on top of the soil.

4.

Cover with a plastic bag (but leave succulents uncovered) to maintain high humidity, keeping it off the leaf and place in a warm location with indirect light Keep the soil moist, but not wet. Water sparingly if needed. Label with the name and the date you did the cutting.

5.

After a few weeks, small plantlets should begin forming at the base of the leaf or along the veins and roots will also have developed. Once the new plantlets are large enough to handle, separate them from the original leaf and transplant into individual pots.

Above Select roots about the thickness of a pencil, cut as close to the plant as possible, insert into a terracotta pot vertically and top with a layer of grit. Label and place in a cold frame.

Root cuttings

Root cuttings are an effective way to propagate plants that don't respond well to stem or leaf cuttings. Using a portion of the plant's root system, you can grow new plants genetically identical to the parent. This method works particularly well for woody or herbaceous perennials, such as phlox, verbascum, blackberry or horseradish. Root cuttings are taken when the plant is dormant, in the autumn or late winter, allowing the plant to focus on generating new shoots and roots. It's a reliable way to increase plant stock while preserving desired characteristics like growth habits or flower colour.

Ingredients

+ Garden spade, fork or hand trowel
+ Garden knife or scissors
+ Rubbing alcohol or a mix of bleach and warm water
+ 9cm (3½in) pot or seed tray with drainage holes, or recycled margarine tub or yoghurt pot
+ Potting compost and perlite or horticultural grit mix
+ Pen
+ Plant label
+ A clear plastic bag (optional)
+ Cold frame (optional)

For thin root cuttings

Insert the cut roots horizontally rather than vertically, lightly cover with soil and finish off with a layer of grit.

1.

Select a healthy, established plant when the plant is dormant, typically in late autumn or early spring.

2.

Use sterilized, sharp tools such as a spade, garden fork or trowel, carefully dig around the plant to expose the roots, taking care not to damage the roots. Gently lift the plant from the soil, exposing the roots.

3.

Choose healthy, thick roots that are at least the diameter of a pencil and using a clean knife or scissors cut these roots cleanly into sections, each about 5–10cm (2–4in) long. Fill a small pot or seed tray with a mix (50:50) of perlite and peat-free compost and moisten the soil. Then insert each root cutting vertically into the soil with the top side facing up and just below the soil surface. A flat cut for the top helps distinguish it, while a slanted cut denotes the bottom, especially useful if you're cutting a long piece of root into sections.

4.

Cover with grit and water them lightly to settle the soil around the roots. Add a label for identification.

5.

You can cover the pot with a plastic bag to maintain humidity. Position the pot in a cold frame or warm area with indirect sunlight and water as needed to keep it consistently damp. Remove the plastic cover occasionally to allow for fresh air and prevent mould.

6.

Patience is key, as it can take several weeks to months for successful rooting, depending on the plant species, but once the new plants have established roots and are growing well, they can be transplanted into larger pots or directly into the garden. Acclimatize them gradually to outdoor conditions if you plan to move them outside.

Layering

Plant layering is a natural propagation method that encourages new plants to grow while still attached to the parent plant, ensuring they receive nutrients until they develop their roots. It works well for plants like roses, rhododendrons, clematis and strawberries. By bending a low-growing branch and covering part of it with soil (either in the ground or in a pot), roots will form at the buried section. Once the new roots are established, the new plant can be separated from the parent. Layering is beneficial because it reduces stress on the cutting, increases the chances of success and produces strong, healthy plants identical to the original.

Ingredients

+ Garden knife or pruning shears
+ 9cm (3½in) pot (optional)
+ Potting compost and horticultural grit (if needed)
+ Rooting hormone compound (optional)
+ A clear plastic bag or homemade cloche from a plastic fizzy-pop bottle (optional)
+ 2 litre (½ gallon) pot (optional)

1.
During the growing season select a healthy, well-watered parent plant with flexible stems low to the ground. Identify a non-flowering stem at least one year old. You can make a small cut or scrape on the underside of the chosen stem about one-third of the way through. This 'wound' encourages root development, particularly if rooting hormone compound is applied. Gently bend the stem 15–30cm (6–8in) down toward the ground keeping it attached to the parent plant.

2.
If using a pot, fill it with a mix of peat-free multi-purpose compost and horticultural grit. If you're layering it in the ground, loosen the soil and make a shallow trench (5–10cm/2–4in deep) and bury the stem (the wounded section if you scraped it ensuring it is in contact with the soil). Firm the soil around the stem to secure it in place.

3.
Water to settle the soil and (optional) cover with a plastic bag or a homemade cloche from a plastic fizzy-pop bottle to maintain humidity. Keep the soil consistently moist.

4.
It may take several weeks to a few months for roots to develop. You can gently tug on the stem to check for resistance, indicating root growth. Once a strong root system has formed, use a clean knife to cut the new rooted plant away from the parent plant and transplant into a larger pot (2-litre) or directly into your garden and water it.

5.
Keep it shaded for a few days to help it acclimatize.

Stake or pin to secure

If the stem is long or to encourage vertical growth, use a stake to hold it upright or secure it with a U-shaped wire (such as a paper clip) or peg.

Division

Plant division is a simple and effective way to propagate many perennial plants, helping rejuvenate older plants while creating new ones. This method involves splitting an established plant into two or more sections, each with its own roots and shoots. Division works well for clumping plants like hostas, irises and daylilies. It helps prevent overcrowding, encourages healthier growth and promotes more vigorous flowering.

Ingredients

- Garden fork or spade
- Knife
- Garden pruners
- Additional peat free compost/ homemade compost

1.

The ideal time for division is in early spring or late autumn when the plant is not actively blooming. Look for a healthy plant that has become overcrowded or has several growth points. Water the plant thoroughly a day or two before dividing it. This will hydrate the roots and make the process easier.

2.

Use a garden fork or spade to carefully dig around the plant 5–10cm (2–4in) away from it and then lift the entire plant out of the ground. Gently shake off or brush away excess soil to expose the root system, so you can see where to make your divisions.

3.

Look for areas where the plant has sent out new shoots or where roots are already separated. Each division should have at least one growing point (stem or bud) and some healthy roots.

4.

Use your hands to gently pull apart the sections. If they are tightly bound, you may need to use a clean knife, pruners or spade to cut through the roots or two forks back-to-back for more established fibrous roots, and trim away any unhealthy roots with your knife or pruners.

5.

Replant the divisions in well-draining soil amended with compost or organic matter either in the ground or in pots. Plant each division at the same depth it was growing before. If it's a clumping plant, space it out appropriately. Firm the soil around each new plant to eliminate air pockets. Water the divisions thoroughly to settle the soil around the roots and apply a layer of mulch around the base of each new plant to help retain moisture and suppress weeds.

6.

Keep an eye on the newly divided plants, ensuring they receive adequate water and protection from extreme sunlight or harsh weather conditions. Be patient, as it may take some time for the divided plants to acclimatize and start growing again.

Above Using a garden fork, dig up your plant, such as this achillea, simply pull apart sections of the plant with a good amount of roots and leaves, then plant the division into a prepared hole. Water it, to settle the soil around the roots.

Offsets

Plant offsets are a straightforward method of propagation that involves separating new shoots or bulbils that develop from the base of a parent plant, or to the side of a bulb. Common in succulents, cacti and some perennials like chives and pinks, offsets can be easily removed and replanted. This method is advantageous because it allows for quick reproduction of genetically identical plants while preserving desirable traits such as flower colour or growth habit. Offsets typically develop root systems, ensuring a higher success rate when transplanted. This efficient technique requires minimal effort and resources, making it ideal if you're looking to expand your collections.

Ingredients

+ Small spade or garden trowel
+ Sharp knife
+ 9cm (3½in) or 1 litre (0.22 gallons) pots or recycled container, such as a yoghurt pot or margarine tub, with drainage holes
+ Potting compost suited to type of plant

1.
Look for small plantlets or offsets near a healthy parent plant's base. Look for ones ready for propagation, which will typically have a few roots and leaves. If already growing in soil, water the parent plant a day or two before taking offsets to ensure that the plant is well-hydrated and to make it easier to separate the offsets.

2.
Using a small spade or garden trowel, carefully separate the bulb offsets or bulbils from the parent plant by gently pulling them apart. Using a sharp knife, trim any damaged or rotted roots.

3.
If you are planting the offsets in pots, fill them with a well-draining potting mix suitable for the type of plant. For succulents and cacti, for example, use a mix (1:1:1) of potting soil, grit or perlite and sand to ensure good drainage.

4.
For bulbils, insert shallowly into soil, but for vegetative offsets, place in a pot with the base of the offset at soil level. Firm the soil gently around the base of the offset to secure it in place and water it.

5.
Place the pots in a location with bright, indirect sunlight and keep an eye on the soil moisture, ensuring it remains slightly moist but not overly wet. Be patient and give the offsets time to grow. It may take several weeks for them to acclimatize and start producing new leaves.

Opposte/Below Remove any excess parts of the tunic, carefully pull off the bulbils or offsets and plant in a recycled plastic container with drainage holes before adding the compost.

Planting

Planting in your garden is a rewarding and fulfilling activity that fosters a connection with nature. It begins with selecting suitable plants and then preparing the soil properly. When it comes to the actual planting, it's essential to allow enough space, and finally, regular watering, mulching and weeding ensure plants thrive so you benefit from beautiful blooms and fresh produce, as well as the joy and health benefits that gardening brings.

The basics

Planting is a fundamental gardening practice that involves establishing plants in soil to grow and flourish. The process begins with careful planning, where you need to consider your garden's climate, soil type and sun exposure. Choosing the right plants is essential, as different species have varying light, water and nutrient requirements.

Preparing the soil before planting is crucial. This involves testing the soil's pH and nutrient levels and amending it with organic matter, such as compost or well-rotted manure, to enhance fertility and improve soil structure. A well-aerated and nutrient-rich soil supports healthy root development and plant growth.

Timing is key when planting. Spring and autumn are typically the best seasons for planting most perennials and annuals, while some crops, like vegetables, may require specific timing based on times when frost is likely. It's important to dig holes that accommodate the plants' root systems, ensuring they are placed at the right depth – usually just deep enough to cover the roots without burying the stem.

Spacing is another critical factor; plants need enough room to grow without competing for resources. Once planted, regular watering, especially in the early stages, is essential for establishment. Mulching helps retain soil moisture and suppress weeds, further supporting plant health. Overall, understanding these basics of planting lays the foundation for a thriving garden, offering both aesthetic beauty and potential harvests for years to come.

Above Find tools that are comfortable to work with. For close up work or tight positions between plants a hand trowel or a short perennial spade are good choices.

When to plant

Timing is crucial in gardening, significantly impacting plant health and productivity. The best time to plant varies, depending on the type of plant and local climate conditions. Generally, spring and autumn are the most favourable seasons for planting many perennials, annuals and shrubs.

Spring planting As the soil warms and the risk of frost diminishes, spring is ideal for planting most flowers and vegetables. Mid-spring to early summer is perfect for sowing seeds directly in the garden or transplanting seedlings. Cool-season crops, such as peas, lettuce and spinach, thrive when planted early in spring, as they can tolerate cooler temperatures.

Autumn planting Early autumn is another excellent time to plant, particularly for perennials, trees and shrubs. The soil is still warm, promoting root growth, while the cooler air temperatures reduce stress on new plants. Aim to plant in early to mid autumn to ensure that roots are established before winter.

Consider local frost dates Knowing your area's average last frost date in spring and first frost date in autumn is vital. Use this information to determine the optimal planting window for your region.

Special cases Some plants, like garlic and certain bulbs, benefit from late autumn planting, allowing them to establish roots before winter.

Ultimately, the key is to understand the specific needs of your plants and your local climate conditions.

Planting your borders

Planting borders is an excellent way to enhance the aesthetic appeal of your garden, create defined spaces and add structure to your landscape. By carefully planning and planting your borders, you can create stunning garden features that thrive throughout the seasons.

Planning your borders Begin by determining the location and size of your border. Consider its purpose – whether it's to separate areas, frame a path or highlight specific plants, for example. Take note of sun and shade patterns and the soil type to help you choose suitable plants.

Selecting plants Choose a mix of perennials, annuals and shrubs that complement each other in colour, height, shape and texture. Consider flowering times to ensure year-round interest. Taller plants should usually be placed at the back of the border, with shorter ones in the front for optimal visibility, although the odd airy tall plant, such as *Verbena bonariensis*, *V. hastata* or *Thalictrum* spp., at the front can add drama and interest. Aim for a mix of mounds and spires and repetition of plants which helps to lead your eye through the border(s).

Above and opposite Mounds and spires create the perfect planting compositions. Use plants repetitively throughout the garden to draw the eye.

Preparing the soil Clear the area of weeds and debris, then loosen the soil to improve aeration. Amend the soil with organic matter, such as compost, to enhance fertility and drainage.

Planting Dig holes for each plant, making sure they are both deep and wide enough to accommodate the root systems. Follow any specific planting guidelines for each plant type. Space the plants appropriately to allow for their mature size.

Watering and mulching After planting, water the border thoroughly to settle the soil. Applying a layer of mulch helps retain moisture and suppress weeds.

Maintenance Regularly check your border for watering needs, weeds and dead or dying foliage. Prune as necessary to encourage healthy growth and shape. Deadhead to prolong flowering.

Planting in pots

This is an ideal solution for those with limited space or poor soil conditions. It allows you to create vibrant displays of flowers, herbs and vegetables in a controlled environment. With proper care, container gardens can flourish, adding beauty and productivity to your space.

Choosing the right pot Select a container appropriate for the plant's size and type. Ensure it has drainage holes to prevent waterlogging. Materials can vary, from terracotta to plastic, each offering unique benefits regarding insulation and weight. When recycling metal or plastic containers, you can add an insulation layer of recycled honeycomb packing paper/cardboard, loose-fill packing chips or polystyrene.

Selecting potting mix Use a high-quality potting mix specifically designed for container gardening. This mix should retain moisture while providing excellent drainage. Avoid using garden soil, which can compact in pots and hinder root growth.

Planting First, add a drainage layer of horticultural grit, broken terracotta pots or (for containers of non-edible plants) recycled polystyrene or plastic pots. Next, fill the pot with the potting mix, leaving about 5cm (2in) of space from the pot's rim. Remove the plant from its nursery container and gently loosen any tightly bound roots. Place the plant in the pot to the same depth as it was growing before. Fill in around the roots with additional potting mix, firming it gently.

Watering After planting, water the pot thoroughly until water drains from the bottom. Monitor the moisture level regularly, as potted plants can dry out faster than those in the ground.

Placement Place the pots according to the plant's light requirements. Some may thrive in full sun, while others prefer partial shade.

Maintenance Regularly fertilize and prune your potted plants to encourage healthy growth.

Top Cardboard can be used to insulate pots, before adding the compost. **Above** Broken pieces of terracotta pots (crocks) cover the drainage hole to prevent soil being washed away.

Planting trees

Planting trees is a rewarding endeavour that contributes to the environment and enhances your garden and the wildlife that you will attract to it. Proper planting techniques are essential for ensuring the tree's health and longevity. With proper care, your tree will thrive and provide benefits for years.

Choose the right tree Select a species suitable for your climate, soil type and available space. Consider the tree's mature size, growth rate and desired aesthetic.

Prepare the site Identify a planting location with adequate sunlight and good drainage. Remove any weeds, grass or debris from the area to minimize competition for resources. If planting a tree in a pot select the right sized pot with drainage holes and consider how long it will remain in this pot.

Digging the hole Dig a hole twice as wide as the tree's root ball and slightly shallower than the ball's height. This encourages roots to spread outward rather than downward. A square hole is also better because it encourages root growth outward, preventing a 'girdling' effect, where roots circle the hole and become constrained.

Inspect the roots Before planting, examine the tree's roots. If they are tightly bound, gently loosen them or make vertical cuts with a knife or sharp spade to encourage outward growth. This is especially important for container-grown trees.

Planting Place the tree in the centre of the hole, ensuring that the top of the root ball is level with or slightly above the surrounding soil. Backfill the hole with the excavated soil, packing it gently to remove air pockets. If growing a tree in a pot, ensure the top of the soil of the nursery pot is a few centimetres below the rim of the final pot.

Watering Water the newly planted tree thoroughly to settle the soil. Continue to water regularly, especially during dry spells.

Mulching and staking Apply a layer of mulch around the base to retain moisture and suppress weeds. If necessary, stake the tree for support, especially in windy areas.

Ongoing care Monitor the tree's health, checking for pests and diseases, and prune as needed to encourage healthy growth.

Above/Opposite Trees can be grown in the ground or a pot. If the latter, remember the tree will need to be repotted regularly to maintain a healthy plant.

Ongoing care and maintenance

Ongoing care and maintenance of a garden are essential for its health and vibrancy. Regular watering is crucial, especially during dry spells, while mulching helps retain moisture and suppress weeds. Pruning encourages growth and removes dead or diseased material. Soil nutrients are boosted by fertilizing with organic compost, supporting plant development. Pest management is vital; monitor for signs of infestation and use natural remedies when possible. Routine weeding will stop competition for resources. Seasonal tasks, such as planting, dividing perennials and preparing for winter, also contribute to a thriving garden year-round. Consistency in care yields beautiful results.

Watering

Watering your garden is a crucial aspect of plant care that directly impacts health and growth. Water is essential for photosynthesis and nutrient transport. It helps maintain cell structure and turgor pressure (the pressure exerted by fluid inside the plant cell), enabling plants to stand upright. Insufficient watering can lead to stress, wilting and reduced growth while overwatering can cause root rot and other diseases. Proper watering promotes a balanced ecosystem, supporting plant health and beneficial soil organisms.

You can create a lush, productive garden by understanding how and why to water effectively. Proper watering techniques and timing can significantly enhance plant vitality. Ideally, collect your rainwater in water butts, troughs or repurposed baths. Water in the early morning or late afternoon to reduce evaporation and ensure plants absorb moisture before the heat of the day. Avoid watering during windy conditions, which can lead to uneven moisture distribution.

Where possible and if your budget permits, use soaker hoses or drip irrigation systems. These efficient methods deliver water directly to the soil, minimizing waste and keeping foliage dry, which prevents fungal diseases. Use a watering can or hose with a spray nozzle for smaller areas.

By watering deeply and less frequently, you encourage roots to grow deeper into the soil, and they are then better equipped to access moisture and nutrients. In other words, watering every day with little water is worse than watering deeply once or twice a week. The latter simply means thoroughly saturating the soil to a depth of several centimetres. Aim for about 3–5cm (1¼ –2in) of water per week, adjusting based on rainfall and plant needs. You can use your finger or a moisture meter to gauge soil dampness. Insert your finger up to the first or second knuckle. If the top 3–5cm (1¼ –2in) feels dry, it's time to water.

Feeding

Feeding your garden enhances soil fertility and provides essential nutrients that support plant functions such as photosynthesis, root development and flowering, and is therefore essential for promoting healthy plant growth, vibrant blooms and bountiful harvests. Proper nutrition helps plants access essential nutrients that support their development and build resilience to environmental stresses and against pests and diseases. Regularly feeding your garden fosters a thriving ecosystem, good for pollinators and beneficial organisms that contribute to a balanced garden environment.

Before adding fertilizers, conduct a soil test to determine nutrient levels and pH. This information helps you choose the right amendments. Next, incorporate organic matter into the soil, such as homemade compost or well-rotted manure, as well as organic mulches such as wood chips or straw. These enrich the soil with nutrients, improve its structure and enhance moisture retention.

Use balanced fertilizers that contain nitrogen (N), phosphorus (P) and potassium (K). These macronutrients are vital for overall plant health. Choose slow-release granular fertilizers for long-lasting effects or liquid fertilizers, such as nettle, seaweed or comfrey, for quick absorption. Apply during the growing season, typically in spring and early summer, when plants are actively developing. Follow the recommended application rates on packages to avoid nutrient burn.

Top Wilted leaves and petals can indicate that a plant needs water. **Above** Homemade feed from nettles can be added to a watering can.

Make your own plant food

Nettles, unfortunately, grow everywhere. Fortunately, you can turn them into a rich plant feed that you can use for edibles and ornamentals, providing your garden with a potent feed. Nettles are packed with essential nutrients like nitrogen, iron, magnesium and potassium, making them an excellent thrifty and organic option for nourishing your plants. Younger plants tend to be richer in nutrients; harvest them in spring or early summer when they are at their most vigorous.

How to use

+ For plants needing a quick nutrient boost, apply the diluted nettle fertilizer directly to the leaves using a sprayer.
+ To promote overall plant health, water the base of your plants with the diluted solution to feed the plant through the roots.

Safety tips

+ Always wear gloves
+ Use in moderation, especially on young plants.
+ Nettle fertilizer has a strong odour, so use it with plenty of fresh air.

Other benefits of nettle fertilizer

+ The strong smell can be a deterrent to certain pests.
+ It can improve soil structure and fertility over time, adding to a healthier garden ecosystem.
+ Making your own fertilizer reduces the need for synthetic options, promoting a more thrifty, sustainable approach.

Ingredients

+ Gloves and scissors (to avoid stings when harvesting and handling nettles)
+ 1kg (just over 2lb) young vigorous nettles (ensure they haven't been treated with pesticides)
+ 10 litres (17½ pints water, preferably rainwater (it's free and free from chemicals found in tap water)
+ Large lidded container (ideally plastic or wood; metal can react with the nettle tea and may corrode)
+ Stirring stick

1.

Wearing gloves, use scissors to cut the nettles; take the top 10–15cm (4–6in), leaving the root system intact so that the plants can regenerate. Snip into small pieces either with scissors or a mower and place in a bucket or container.

2.

Add the chopped nettles to the container with the water, so that the nettles are fully submerged and the container about two-thirds full. Cover with a lid to minimize the smell, which can be pretty potent and place it in a shaded spot in your garden and let the mixture steep.

3.

The fermentation process typically takes between two to three weeks, depending on the temperature. Stir the mixture every few days to help release the nutrients.

4.

Strain the liquid to remove the plant material, which can be composted. The concentrated liquid can now be used as a fertilizer. Dilute it at a ratio of 1:10 (one part nettle fertilizer to ten parts water) for general feeding. It is best used fresh but can be stored for several weeks.

Above Remove the nettles using pruners, avoiding the roots. Cut into smaller pieces and place in a bucket. Submerge in water, cover with a lid and leave to steep.

Mulching

Mulching serves several vital purposes in your garden. It involves applying a material layer over the soil surface and offers numerous advantages for plant health and soil management, reducing maintenance efforts and contributing to a thriving ecosystem. It helps retain soil moisture by reducing evaporation, which is particularly beneficial during dry spells. Additionally, mulch suppresses weed growth, minimizing competition for nutrients and light. As organic mulches, such as wood chips, homemade compost, straw or shredded leaves, break down, they enrich the soil with essential nutrients, promoting healthy plant growth. Furthermore, mulching moderates soil temperature, keeping roots cooler in the summer and warmer in the winter – like a winter duvet. Inorganic options, like gravel or landscape fabric, provide long-lasting coverage without adding nutrients.

Before applying mulch, clear the area of weeds and debris. Ensure that the soil is moist, as mulch helps retain moisture. Spread a layer of mulch 5–10cm (2–4in) thick around plants, keeping it a little way away from plant stems to prevent rot. For larger areas, use a rake to create an even layer. Regularly check your mulch, replenishing it to maintain the desired depth and effectiveness. Remove any weeds that grow through the mulch layer or where birds have dropped weed seeds.

Above Bark chippings are the perfect mulch.

Opposite Prune when plants are dormant in the autumn or late spring/summer for early flowering shrubs and trees.

Pruning

Pruning plants contributes significantly to your garden's health, appearance and productivity. It encourages new growth by removing dead, diseased or damaged branches. This allows the plant to direct its energy toward healthier parts, promoting vigorous growth and improving overall vitality.

Thinning out overcrowded branches increases airflow within the plant. Better air circulation reduces humidity, which helps prevent fungal diseases and pest infestations. This is particularly important in dense plants where moisture can linger and lead to rot. Pruning also allows sunlight to reach the inner parts of the plant. This is crucial for flowering and fruiting plants, as it ensures that all parts receive adequate light, promoting even growth and better yields. Regular pruning helps maintain a desired shape and size for ornamental plants, shrubs and trees. This not only improves your garden's visual appeal but also prevents plants from becoming overgrown and unruly.

Many flowering and fruiting plants benefit from strategic pruning, as it can stimulate the production of blooms and fruits. Removing old or spent flowers (deadheading) encourages new blooms while pruning fruit trees can enhance fruit quality and quantity. Pruning is, therefore, essential for maintaining plant health, aesthetics and productivity. It fosters a thriving garden environment, ensuring that plants survive and flourish over time.

How to prune

Pruning is a critical gardening technique that enhances plant health, encourages growth and improves overall aesthetics. Follow these steps as a guide to how to prune your plants effectively, ensuring they remain healthy and attractive throughout the growing season.

Know when to prune Timing varies depending on the plant type. Late winter or early spring is ideal for deciduous trees and shrubs, as they are still dormant. Spring-flowering plants should be pruned right after blooming to avoid cutting off next year's buds. Summer-blooming varieties can be pruned in late winter or early spring.

Gather your tools Ensure you have the right tools: use sharp pruning shears for small branches, loppers for medium-sized branches and a pruning saw for larger limbs. Clean tools after use with rubbing alcohol to prevent disease transmission.

Assess the plant Examine the plant and identify dead, damaged or diseased branches. Also, look for overcrowded or crossing branches that hinder air circulation and light penetration.

Make strategic cuts Start by removing dead or damaged wood. Then thin out crowded areas to improve airflow. When pruning, make clean cuts at a 45-degree angle, just above a bud or node, angled away from the bud or node, to promote healthy regrowth. Avoid leaving stubs.

Shape and size Shape the plant by cutting back long, leggy growth and maintaining a balanced structure. Step back periodically to evaluate your work and ensure a harmonious shape.

Clean up Collect and dispose of cuttings to reduce the risk of spreading pests and diseases.

Above/Opposite Thicker branches should be removed using loppers or a garden saw. Ensure you keep your blades clean at all times. Secateurs are perfect for everyday pruning.

Diseases, pests and prevention

Maintaining a healthy garden requires vigilance against the diseases (caused by fungi, bacteria or viruses) and pests threatening plant vitality. Understanding common issues and implementing preventive measures is key to promoting a thriving garden ecosystem.

Fungal infections, such as powdery mildew and root rot, thrive in damp conditions, which are often exacerbated by poor air circulation. Bacterial diseases, like bacterial wilt, can quickly spread through water or soil. Identifying symptoms early – such as wilting, yellowing leaves or unusual spots – allows prompt intervention.

Insects, including aphids, spider mites and whiteflies, can inflict damage by sucking sap from plants or transmitting diseases. Larger pests, like slugs and snails, may chew through leaves and stems, weakening the plant.

Prevention strategies

Reduce the risk of diseases and pests and foster a healthy and productive garden environment, by proactively using the following strategies.

Cultural practices Improve airflow and reduce humidity by spacing plants properly. Rotate crops annually to disrupt pest and disease cycles.

Healthy soil Maintain healthy soil through composting and regular testing to ensure optimal nutrient levels. Healthy plants are more resilient to diseases and pests.

Companion planting These techniques help deter pests. For example, planting marigolds can repel nematodes and harmful insects.

Regular monitoring Frequently inspect plants for early signs of trouble. Hand-picking larger pests off your plants and removing infected leaves can prevent larger outbreaks.

Natural remedies Utilize organic pest control methods, such as insecticidal soap or neem oil, to minimize chemical use while effectively managing pests.

Caring for the rest of your garden

Caring for the non-plant elements, which all contribute to your garden's overall health and enjoyment, is essential for creating a functional and aesthetically pleasing outdoor space. Maintain and take care of structures, pathways and garden accessories to enhance the beauty and functionality of your garden and create an enjoyable space for relaxation and recreation.

Pathways Regularly inspect and maintain pathways to ensure they remain safe and accessible. Remove weeds, debris and overgrown vegetation that may encroach on walking areas. If using gravel or mulch, replenish it to maintain a clean appearance. Keep edging materials, like bricks or stones, intact to define borders clearly.

Garden furniture Keep garden furniture clean and in good condition. To prolong its lifespan, regularly wipe down surfaces and protect furniture during harsh weather. Apply protective coatings or treatments to wooden items to prevent rot and decay.

Water features If your garden includes ponds or fountains, check for algae growth and clean them regularly to maintain water quality. Ensure that pumps and filters function correctly to keep water circulating and prevent stagnation.

Tools Store gardening tools in a clean, dry place. Regularly inspect them for wear and tear, sharpen blades and clean rust to extend their life.

The compost area Compost bins should be maintained by regularly turning the material to promote decomposition. To create a tidy garden environment, ensure waste is managed properly, whether through composting or recycling.

Make your own pesticides and herbicides

Rather than buying commercial pesticides, create natural alternatives using common kitchen ingredients.. This is not only cost-effective but also avoids the use of harmful chemicals.

Ingredients

- Washing up liquid
- Neem oil
- Milk
- Bicarbonate of soda
- White vinegar
- Sugar

General pesticide

Mix 100 parts water, a big squirt of washing up liquid and 1 part neem oil and spray directly onto plants to help control pests such as aphids, caterpillars, thrips and spider mites

Mildew treatment

Mix milk and water, in a 50:50 ratio, and spray onto plants to treat powdery mildew. Wipe off any residual milk sitting on leaves or flowers after 30 minutes with a dry cloth. The plant will absorb the rest, adding calcium and B vitamins, which are beneficial, especially for blossom-end rot in tomatoes or squashes.

PH herbicide

Mix 10g (1/3 oz) of bicarbonate of soda in 400ml (13½fl oz) of water and spray your plants for healthy leaves, by raising the pH level on leaf surfaces, making it difficult for fungal diseases like powdery mildew and black spot to thrive.

Natural bug deterrent

Mix 20g (2/3 oz) of bicarbonate of soda in 350ml (12fl oz) of water and add 30ml (1fl oz) of white vinegar. Spray your plants as a natural bug deterrent.

General herbicide

Mix 30g (1oz) of bicarbonate of soda and 30g (1oz) of sugar in 350 ml (12fl oz) of water and spray your plants to keep powdery mildew and other fungal diseases away.

SEASONAL TASKS

Seasonal tasks are essential for maintaining a healthy and thriving garden throughout the year. Prepare the soil in spring by tilling and adding compost, then planting seeds and young plants. Summer tasks include regular watering, weeding and deadheading flowers to encourage blooms. In autumn, focus on harvesting crops, cleaning up debris and planting perennials or bulbs for spring. Winter is a time for assessing your garden, pruning dormant plants and protecting sensitive species from harsh weather.

Spring

Spring is a vibrant time in the garden, marked by new growth and a surge of activity. As the days grow longer and temperatures rise, several essential tasks can help ensure your garden thrives throughout the growing season.

Soil preparation As soon as the soil is workable, begin preparing it for planting. Clear away any debris from winter, such as fallen leaves and dead plant material. Then, test the soil to determine its pH (see page 29) and nutrient levels. Amend the soil with organic matter, like homemade compost or well-rotted manure, to improve its structure and fertility. This step is crucial for creating a healthy foundation for your plants.

Above A spring display of *Iris reticulata* adds colour early on in the year

Planting seeds and seedlings Once the danger of frost has passed, you can start sowing seeds directly into the garden. Cool-season crops like peas, lettuce and radishes thrive in the cooler temperatures of early spring. For tender plants such as tomatoes, peppers and basil, begin indoors or purchase seedlings from a nursery to transplant later. Ensure you follow the recommended planting depths and spacing for each variety.

Weeding Spring is the perfect time to tackle weeds before they take over. Regularly check your garden for early signs of invasive plants and remove them promptly. Hand-pulling weeds or using a hoe can prevent them from seeding and spreading. Mulching around plants can also help suppress weeds while retaining soil moisture.

Pruning and deadheading Pruning is essential in spring, especially for flowering shrubs and trees. Remove dead or damaged branches to encourage new growth and improve air circulation. Cut back growth left on over the winter. Deadhead spent flowers on perennials and annuals to promote continued blooming throughout the season.

Fertilizing Feed your plants a balanced fertilizer to provide the nutrients they need for vigorous growth. Organic options, like compost tea (a liquid fertilizer made by steeping compost in water) or nettle fertilizer (see pages 168–9), can nourish your plants without the risk of chemical build-up.

Watering and irrigation Monitor soil moisture levels and ensure your plants receive adequate water as temperatures rise. Consider setting up a drip irrigation system or soaker hoses to provide consistent moisture, especially for newly planted seedlings, reducing the amount of water you use and saving on your water bills.

Completing these spring gardening jobs will set the stage for a lush and productive garden. Embracing the energy of spring will help you cultivate a thriving outdoor space to enjoy throughout the warmer months.

Top left Seedlings will be growing. **Top right** Bare root or root-balled trees, such as these espaliered hornbeams, need to be planted between November and March. **Above** Weeds will be growing, so start early and keep on top of them.

Summer

Summer is a time of growth and abundance in the garden, requiring specific tasks to ensure plants remain healthy and productive. The long days and warm temperatures create ideal conditions for various gardening activities.

Watering wisely As temperatures rise, consistent watering becomes crucial. Aim to water deeply and less frequently, with collected rainwater, to encourage deep root growth. Early morning is the best time to water, as it reduces evaporation and allows foliage to dry before evening, helping to prevent fungal diseases. If budget allows, consider using soaker hoses or drip irrigation systems to deliver moisture directly to the soil, minimizing waste.

Above Take time out from gardening and just look at what's going on. Observation is key for detecting pests and diseases.

Weeding regularly Weeds can thrive in the summer heat, competing for nutrients and water. Make it a habit to inspect your garden weekly for weeds. Hand-pulling or using a hoe can help control them before they go to seed. Apply a layer of mulch around your plants to suppress weed growth and to help retain soil moisture.

Fertilizing Summer is critical for feeding your plants, especially flowering and fruiting varieties. Use a balanced fertilizer or compost to provide the nutrients your plants need. Be cautious not to over-fertilize, as this can lead to excessive leaf growth at the expense of flowers and fruits. Regularly check the nutrient levels of your soil to adjust your feeding routine accordingly.

Pruning and pinching While spring is often associated with pruning, summer offers additional maintenance opportunities. Pinching back leggy growth on annuals and perennials encourages bushier plants and more blooms. Removing spent flowers (deadheading) promotes continuous flowering and prevents plants from going to seed too early.

Pest and disease management Monitor your garden for signs of pests and diseases regularly. Common summer pests include aphids, spider mites and caterpillars. Use natural pest control methods, such as introducing beneficial insects like ladybirds or insecticidal soap. Additionally, look out for any signs of disease, such as yellowing leaves or unusual spots, and address issues promptly to minimize damage.

Harvesting Summer is the season for bountiful harvests. Regularly check your vegetable garden for ripe produce and harvest promptly to encourage further growth. Frequent harvesting can prevent plants from becoming overripe and help maintain optimal flavour and texture.

Stay on top of these summer gardening jobs to ensure your garden remains vibrant, productive and healthy throughout the warm months. Embrace the summer so you can enjoy the fruits of your labour while creating a lush sanctuary.

Top left Pinching out encourages bushier growth. **Top right** Start havesting potatoes. **Above** Continue weeding, using a hoe for larger areas. Use a back and forth motion on a warm day and leave the 'severed' weeds on the soil surface to wither and die.

Autumn

Autumn is a critical time in the garden, as it marks the transition from the vibrant summer activity to the quiet dormancy of winter. It's essential to complete specific tasks during this season to prepare your garden for the colder months and set the stage for a successful spring.

Harvesting crops As the growing season ends, it's time to reap the rewards of your hard work. Harvest vegetables, fruits and herbs before the first frost. Regularly picking crops like tomatoes, peppers and squash prevents overripening and encourages further growth. Don't forget to gather any remaining herbs, which can be dried or frozen for use throughout the winter.

Cleaning up debris Remove dead or diseased plant material from your garden beds. This helps prevent pests and diseases from overwintering in your garden. Compost healthy plant material, but dispose of any diseased plants in the rubbish bin to avoid spreading pathogens. Clearing away fallen leaves and debris also improves air circulation and prepares the soil for winter. Remember, you can make your own lead mould (see page 40).

Soil preparation Autumn is an ideal time to amend your soil. Conduct a soil test to determine nutrient levels and pH (see page 29). Based on the results, add organic matter, such as homemade compost or well-rotted manure, to enrich the soil. Tilling (or turning over) the soil also helps incorporate these amendments and break up compacted areas, promoting better drainage and root penetration in spring.

Planting perennials and bulbs Planting perennials and spring-flowering bulbs, such as tulips and daffodils, during autumn allows them to establish roots before the ground freezes. Choose a sunny location and follow each variety's recommended planting depths and spacing.

Pruning While heavy pruning is typically reserved for late winter or early spring, autumn is an excellent time to remove dead or diseased branches. This encourages healthy growth and reduce the risk of fungal diseases.

Mulching Applying a layer of mulch around plants provides insulation and helps regulate soil temperature. Organic mulches also suppress weeds and retain moisture. Aim for a layer of 5–10cm (2–4in), ensuring it doesn't touch plant stems to prevent rot.

Winter protection As temperatures drop, consider protecting tender plants from frost. Use row covers, cloches or hessian/burlap to shield vulnerable species. For perennials, you can apply a layer of mulch or leaves to insulate the roots.

Completing these autumn gardening jobs will ensure that your garden remains healthy and prepared for the winter months as well as leading to a more vibrant garden when spring arrives.

Top Adding grit to heavy soil improves structure and drainage. **Above left** Homemade compost can be added to mulch pots and borders or to improve the stucture of heavy or sandy soils. **Above right** Autumn is bulb planting time. **Opposite** Removing dead branches in autumn encourages growth.

Winter

Winter may seem like a dormant period in the garden, but it presents an opportunity for essential maintenance and preparation for the upcoming growing season. Engaging in specific winter gardening jobs can help ensure a healthy and vibrant garden in spring.

Clean and organize tools Winter is an ideal time to clean and sharpen your gardening tools. Remove dirt and debris from shovels, pruners and trowels, and wipe them down with a cloth to prevent rust. Sharpen blades using a sharpening stone to ensure they're ready for spring tasks. Organizing your tools in a designated space will streamline your gardening efforts when the growing season begins.

Protect tender plants If you have tender plants that may not withstand freezing temperatures, consider providing protection. Use hessian/burlap or row covers to shield them from frost. Move plants in pots to a sheltered area close to the wall of the house, or indoors if possible. Mulching around the base of plants helps insulate the roots and retain moisture.

Plan for spring Winter is the perfect time to reflect on your garden's successes and challenges during the preceding seasons. Refer to your gardening journal (see page 49), note which plants thrived and which didn't, and use this information to plan your garden layout for the next growing season. Consider experimenting with new plant varieties or more companion plants to improve your garden's overall health.

Maintain soil health While the ground may be frozen, there are still things you can do to improve soil health. Conduct a soil test to assess nutrient levels and pH (see page 29). Based on the results, plan to amend the soil with homemade compost or organic fertilizers in the spring. Additionally, consider covering soil with a winter cover crop, like clover or vetch, to prevent erosion and improve soil fertility (see pages 40–41 and 167).

Prune dormant plants Late winter is an excellent time to prune certain trees and shrubs, as pruning while the plants are dormant minimizes stress and encourages vigorous regrowth when spring arrives. Focus on removing dead, damaged or crossing branches to promote healthy growth.

Winter interest Enhance your garden's aesthetics during the winter months by incorporating evergreens and plants with interesting bark or berries. Arrange outdoor decorations or create a winter garden theme to maintain visual interest throughout the season.

Prepare for seed starting As winter progresses, start gathering materials you need to start your seeds. Organize seed packets, gather pots and consider a suitable indoor space with adequate light. By preparing early, you can jump-start your garden in spring.

You can maintain a productive garden ecosystem by actively engaging in these winter gardening jobs, ensuring it's primed and ready for a flourishing spring. Embrace the season as an opportunity for preparation, planning and nurturing your gardening space.

Opposite Protect more tender plants with hessian sacks. Leave seedheads for winter interest and clean your tools thoroughly, ready for next year.

Troubleshooting

Gardening is a rewarding endeavour, but it often comes with its share of challenges. Troubleshooting issues in the garden is crucial for maintaining plant health and ensuring a bountiful harvest.

Identifying pest problems

Common pests Insects such as aphids, caterpillars, slugs and spider mites can wreak havoc on your plants.

Symptoms Look for holes in leaves, sticky residue (honeydew), webbing or visible insects on the plants. Yellowing or wilting leaves may also indicate pest damage.

Solutions For larger pests like caterpillars, hand-picking them off your plants can be effective. Introduce beneficial insects such as ladybirds and lacewings, which feed on common pests. Use insecticidal soap, an eco-friendly option that suffocates soft-bodied insects. Spray in the early morning or late evening to avoid harming beneficial insects or use neem oil, a natural pesticide that disrupts the life cycle of pests without harming beneficial insects when used correctly (see pages 174–5).

Addressing disease issues

Common diseases Fungal diseases like powdery mildew, root rot and blight are prevalent in gardens.

Symptoms Look for signs such as yellowing leaves, black spots, wilting or unusual growths. Fungal diseases may present as white, powdery coatings on leaves.

Solutions Ensure proper air circulation around plants and avoid overhead watering, which can promote fungal growth. Remove and dispose of infected plant debris to prevent the spread of disease. Clean tools regularly to avoid transferring pathogens. Use organic fungicides like sulphur or copper-based sprays for treatment, applying them as soon as symptoms are noticed.

Soil problems

Common soil issues Poor drainage, compacted soil or nutrient deficiencies can impact plant growth.

Symptoms Signs of poor soil conditions include stunted growth, yellowing leaves or wilting plants despite adequate watering.

Solutions Conduct a soil test to identify nutrient levels and pH. Based on the test results, amend the soil with organic matter, such as homemade compost, to improve structure and fertility. If drainage is an issue, consider adding sand or peat-free multi-purpose compost to enhance aeration. Apply a layer of organic mulch around plants to retain moisture and regulate soil temperature, reducing compaction over time.

Watering issues

Common watering problems Overwatering or underwatering can lead to serious plant health issues.

Symptoms Signs of overwatering include yellowing leaves, wilting or root rot. Underwatered plants may show signs of drooping, crisping or leaf drop.

Solutions Establish a regular watering schedule based on your plants' needs and the weather.

Early morning is the best time for watering to minimize evaporation. Use your finger or a moisture meter to check soil moisture before watering. Soil should be moist but not soggy. Ensure pots and garden beds have proper drainage to prevent waterlogging. Raised beds can help improve drainage in heavy soils.

Sunlight Issues

Common light problems Plants may not receive the appropriate sunlight, leading to weak growth.

Symptoms Signs of inadequate light include leggy growth, yellowing leaves or flowers that fail to bloom.

Solutions Understand the light needs of each plant species in your garden. Most vegetables and flowering plants require full sun (6–8 hours per day) for optimal growth. If possible, move potted plants to sunnier locations or trim back overgrown plants that may be shading others. For indoor plants, consider using grow lights to provide adequate illumination.

Nutrient deficiencies

Common deficiencies Nutrient shortages, particularly nitrogen, phosphorus and potassium, can affect plant health.

Symptoms Yellowing leaves indicate nitrogen deficiency, purple leaves indicate phosphorus deficiency and poor fruit development indicates potassium deficiency.

Solutions Apply balanced fertilizers based on soil test results. Organic options like compost or well-rotted manure provide slow-release nutrients. For quick nutrient uptake, consider foliar feeding, where diluted liquid fertilizers are sprayed directly onto leaves. Practise crop rotation to enhance soil fertility and reduce pest and disease build-up.

Seasonal adjustments

Adapting to seasonal changes Seasonal shifts can also pose challenges in the garden, requiring adjustments.

Symptoms Plants may struggle to thrive as temperatures rise or fall, affecting growth and bloom cycles.

Solutions Choose varieties suited to your local climate and seasonal changes. Use more heat-tolerant plants in summer and more cold-hardy varieties in winter. Use row covers to protect plants from frost in early spring and extend the growing season in autumn.

Planning for the future

Continuous learning Gardening is a process of trial and error. Keep a gardening journal to track successes and failures, noting what works and what doesn't (see page 49).

Community resources Engage with local gardening groups for advice and support. Many communities offer workshops, seminars and resources for troubleshooting gardening issues.

By being proactive and observant, you can effectively troubleshoot problems in your garden, ensuring your plants remain healthy and vibrant. Embrace each challenge as a learning opportunity, and remember that even experienced gardeners face difficulties. With patience and persistence, you can cultivate a thriving garden that provides joy and nourishment year after year.

Index

About the author

Mark Lane is a multi-award-winning garden designer, horticulturalist, gardener, author and television presenter, well-known for his appearances on BBC One's *Morning Live*, BBC Two's *Gardeners' World*, and the BBC's coverage of the RHS Flower Shows. He has also appeared on popular programmes such as *Celebrity Mastermind*, *Pointless Celebrities* and *Celebrity Weakest Link*. Other credits include *Prue Leith's Cotswold Kitchen* on ITV and Channel 5's *Royal Homes* and *Royal Gardens*.

Mark was listed in the top 100 people in horticulture in 2025 by *HortWeek*. He has been recognized on the Shaw Trust's Disability Power 100 list in 2023, nominated as Celebrity of the Year at the National Diversity Awards in 2021, and awarded an Honorary Doctorate by the University of Kent in 2022. His practice, Mark Lane Designs Ltd, has received multiple national awards for excellence in landscape architecture and design.

Mark is also an ambassador for several national charities, including the National Trust, Melanoma Fund, Thrive and Gardening with Disabilities Trust.

His published works include *Royal Gardens of the World* (Kyle Books, 2020) and *The Future of Gardens* (Melville House, 2025). He writes regularly for the national and horticultural press.

Acknowledgements

Writing *The Thrifty Gardener* has been a journey shaped by the generosity, inspiration and encouragement of many people. First and foremost, my heartfelt thanks go to my husband Jasen, whose patience, love and constant support gave me the confidence to bring this book to life.

I am deeply grateful to the gardening community – from fellow designers and passionate home gardeners to allotment keepers and community groups – who continue to prove that creativity flourishes even on the tightest of budgets. Their ingenuity and warm conversations have been a constant source of ideas and motivation.

Thanks must also go to the publishers, editors and designers who have guided this project with care and professionalism, and to the photographer Sarah Cuttle whose work adds such richness to my words.

Lastly, I want to thank every reader who chooses to garden thriftily. By reusing, recycling and reimagining, you show that beautiful, sustainable gardens rich in biodiversity can be created by reducing waste and spending wisely, and your efforts are what truly make this book meaningful.